THE COMPLETE
GUIDE DOG FOR THE BLIND

The Complete Guide Dog for the Blind

Robbie Robson

OLDENBURG VERLAG
Carlisle

OLDENBURG VERLAG LTD
1 Palmer Road
Carlisle CA2 7NE

Robbie Robson asserts the
moral right to be identified
as the author of this work.

A CIP catalogue record for
this book is available from
the British Library

ISBN 1 900344 00 9

Printed in Great Britain by
Charles Thurnam and Sons Ltd.
Lonsdale Street, Carlisle.

CONTENTS

FIGURES   Page

PREFACE

Humans enjoy reflective thought; they can look back on the past, consider the present, and project into the future. Animals are beings of the moment, the here and now. Animals cannot reason. Animals, including dogs, are incapable of symbolic thought and react primarily to stimuli in a manner pre-determined by a diversity of conditioned responses or innate reflex activity. Yet dogs are trusting, agreeable, biddable, companionable, cuddlesome, attractive, playful creatures, and display simple affinity with, and affection for, humankind of all descriptions.

They have a good memory, are servile, and require little care since they are satisfied with the basics of life. It is because the dog has a retentive memory which fosters, through repetition, the mechanistic capacity to respond to various stimuli, that it can be trained to perform a multitude of tasks. One of these tasks is a guide for a blind person.

Guide dog training becomes particularly complex because of the ultimate interaction between canine and blind handler, preceding which is the training of the former - with the latter in mind – followed by the tuition of the two together. To be taken into consideration, therefore, is not only the temperament and practical capabilities of the dog but, to an even greater degree, the psychosocial composition and physical and verbal skills of the blind person, not to mention his environmental surrounds.

The dog is therefore a means to an end; a means to enhance the mobility and safety and independence of a visually handicapped person, and at the same time provide him with a well-behaved and socially acceptable canine companion, and the outcome, to be idealistic, is a human being functioning at a higher level of practical ability and free pedestrian travel at a safe and comfortable pace. In turn, these increased personal skills now bring about a greater self assurance and composure in the blind person, thus emphasising the not inconsiderable part guide dog ownership can play in enhancing social and emotional relationships on a wide scale.

On the debit side, where a blind person undertakes training with a guide dog and failure ensues, the damage to the student's esteem can be - albeit without foundation and justification - not only considerable but sometimes lasting. Guide dog training is therefore not to be embarked upon lightly, and the blind applicant should be

9

comprehensively assessed as to his chances of success or failure by a qualified professional.

At the same time, every effort should be made to allocate even a seemingly ineffectual applicant with a guide dog, since if this is the sort of mobility aid he has set his sights on, it would be wrong to flippantly deny it to him. In other words, only where candidates who will clearly fail the course of training present themselves, should the opportunity of guide dog ownership be denied them.

PART ONE: CANIS FAMILIARIS

"His faithful dog shall bear him company".
Alexander Pope (1688-1744)

1

ORIGINS AND DEVELOPMENT OF GUIDE DOGS FOR THE BLIND

Oh what should I do for a dog?
Of sight I have not a particle,
  Globe, Standard, or *Sun,*
  Times, Chronicle - none
Can give *me* a good leading article.

A Mastiff once led me about,
But people appeared so to fear him
  I might have got pence
  Without his defence,
But Charity would not come near him....

A foxhound once served me as guide,
A good one at hill, and at valley;
  But day after day
  He led me astray,
To follow a milk-woman's tally....

A Pointer once pointed my way,
But did not turn out quite so pleasant
  At each hour I'd a stop
  At a poulterers's shop
To point at a very high pheasant....

Lament of a Poor Blind, Thomas Hood (1799-1845)

The special relationship which exists between man and dog reaches a remarkable zenith when the subordinate animal is cast in the role of guide for a blind person. Emphasis is laid upon the description subordinate since, although to the casual onlooker the dog may seem to be the dominant and controlling partner of this workmanlike team of man and animal, on the contrary it is the human element who wields supreme authority, an authority without which the capability and safety of the two would, at the most be lost, and at the least suffer adversely. If, therefore, as is the wont of the bystander to laud the praises of the dog, even further must he laud the praises of the handler.

Many years, many centuries ago, plaudits would have been lavished even more profusely upon the guide dog user of those far-off days, since, unlike nowadays when the animals are supplied through organisations which professionally train them for the specific purpose of guiding, it was at the hands of the owner that the animal was trained. Often, through a mix of trial and error, unsophisticated human skill and endeavour, and indeterminate canine initiative and sagacity, a resolute and worthwhile partnership between man and dog would result, giving some measure of mobility and independence to the blind person who confidently followed, at the end of a lead, the quadruped which he had successfully trained to act as his guide. But just as often, in other less-productive partnerships, trouble, trauma, disharmony and perhaps even disaster, would ensue. A rather sardonic yet often cuttingly factual poem by Thomas Hood perhaps over-emphasises but nevertheless pinpoints the difficulties faced by, in the days of yester-year, the blind person who sought to train his own guide dog. But train his own dog he must, if indeed such a guide he needed - although more often it would be used as an adjunct to mendicancy. And because of the lack of human escorts willing to expend time and forbearance in accompanying him, a dog was the only alternative.

To set a date as to when man first made use of a guide dog, or to endeavour to place the scenario for this momentous event, one might as well attempt to do the same for the invention of the wheel. That many blind people made use of self-trained guide dogs over the ages is, however, apparent. We gather this from the representation of a blind man with a guide dog found painted on the wall of a house in Pompeii, which in 79 A.D. was covered in volcanic ash, to be disclosed when excavation took place at a much later date. A 13th century Chinese scroll also shows a blind man with a dog. An English monk, Bartholomew, domiciled in France, makes mention of a blind man being led by a guide dog, and dates his notes 1260. It is also chronicled that St. Herve, who lived in Brittany in the sixth century, was blind and used a dog as a guide.

King Odran, ruler of a province in Germany, and who reigned some 100 years before Christ was born, made use of a guide dog. A 1465 woodcut showing a blind man being led by a dog - as always, on a lead as opposed to the rigid handle and harness employed nowadays - is also a German representation. In *Henry IV part two* Shakespeare makes reference to a dog leading a blind person. Many artists of the 16th and 17th centuries paint blind users of guide dogs; Callot, Peter Nip, Van de Venne, Bellange and Rembrandt notably.

In his *Blind Man on the Bridge* Thomas Gainsborough (1727-1788) shows the subject of his painting being led by a guide dog. Bigg, Browne and Parry are other English artists who depict similar scenes in the next century. Thomas Bewick, in *A General History of Quadrupeds* (1790) not only illustrates a gentleman with a guide dog, but writes a glowing paragraph about "this creature's sagacity.... in directing the steps of the blind man."

Other European artists of the period who portray guide dogs include Tintoretto, Bombleid, Wafflard, Charlet, Dore, Roehm, Grenier, Motte, Delpek, Langendyk, Duval, Adam and Alophe. The last-named French artist, in a particularly fine woodcut, shows a man and his wife, both blind, being led by a large spaniel (present-day techniques of guide dog training mitigate against more than one person being led by the individual dog which has been specifically trained and assigned to that particular person. Alophe's subjects would therefore each be allocated with a dog rather than struggling along with one guide dog between two, which could prove to be a difficult practice). A Paris engraving of 1801 by George Willie shows two blind beggars, each being led by a dog, passing each other on a path. Most of the dogs illustrated in the drawings described are often of an indeterminate breed, and indeed are usually mongrels. Of course, as well as being unsophisticated guide dogs, these animals would additionally serve as companions and protectors. Sometimes, in fact, their protective qualities might get the better of them, as witness the mastiff in Hood's poem.

In the Perkins Library, Boston, Massachusetts, is to be found a book dated 1843 in which a picture is described by the caption "The blind man by his faithful dog is led". Also in the United States, written evidence of early owner-trained guide dogs is provided by Abram Courtney who, in 1856, detailed his methods of training a spaniel cross to become his escort and mentor. Courtney writes: "My faithful dog, Caper, leads me around corners and across streets, always appraising me of approaching danger.... he has accompanied me in my travels through nearly all of the Northern States; and has served me in the capacity of guide, companion, bodyguard and monitor."

Joseph Reisinger, born in Austria in 1755, became totally blind at the age of 17. Asked by a friend why he didn't train a dog to serve as his guide, he was thus inspired to set about the task. An article, again in the Perkins Library, relates how he went about training a dog to become his guide, although not without accident and incident before reaching a successful conclusion. But once completed, "The training which he had given the dog was such that the dog would always take him up to an entrance or stairs and stand in front of a door until his master had transacted his business, and it is notable that the dog was also careful never himself to go under partially lowered gates which would have bumped his master."

This dog was a Spitz which lived until it was 16 years old. But before that Reisinger was busily preparing a younger animal to replace the old dog, this time a poodle which, apparently, was quick to learn and indeed turned out to be a better guide than its predecessor. "This poodle was so faithful to his master that he was never distracted from his work by other dogs nor was he tempted by proffered bones but should he, doglike, be in the slightest distracted, a slight pull on the leash would bring him back to duty."

After 13 years as a guide this dutiful poodle died in 1809. Again, Reisinger, with forethought, was training a third dog to follow in the footsteps of the poodle. This dog, the largest of the three, gave 14 years of loyal service to Reisinger, who now, with advancing age, resigned himself to a more sedentary life.

Perhaps inspired by the successes of Reisinger in using a dog as a guide, and having noted his training methods, a fellow Austrian, Wilhelm Klein, in 1819 wrote a *Textbook for Teaching the Blind* in which he says: "In an institute for the blind, dogs can also be prepared to serve as guides to such of the blind as are accustomed to walk about. From the collar of the dog extends either a strap or a stick which is grasped by the left hand of the blind person, who also uses a cane in the right hand."

Significantly, here we have first mention of a rigid attachment – a stick - to the collar of the dog, which proved to be the prototype, although now much modified, of the modern harness handle. In the 19th century carrying a cane in the guide dog user's right hand is also recommended. Nowadays, except in the case of additionally incapacitated or elderly guide dog owners this practice is not common. Klein goes on to say that "The training of the dogs, at least in the beginning, must be done by a sighted person.... Then the blind person takes the dog in hand himself and goes with him in order to become accustomed to the movements and signals of the animal. It is obvious that from now on the dog will be fed and cared for by the blind person himself, in order to arrive at a mutual understanding and to establish a true and faithful attachment with the leader dog."

In 1840, Jacob Birrer, a blind Bavarian, published his biography in which he describes the training of guide dogs. He writes: "Probably among all the domestic animals that serve man there is none which performs as many services as the dog .... Especially for the blind the animal performs most effective services: he functions excellently for those who have been robbed of their eyesight .... But for this he ought to be trained with special care by the blind person himself. I feel it a duty therefore to my blind colleagues who want to be guided by dogs, to give instructions, based largely on my own practical experiences, for training the dogs. Some four or five years ago I learned that in Paris many a blind person has a poodle as a guide, but I could not entirely believe it. At that time I did not want a dog as a guide; but about two years ago I had the idea that I would try an experiment with a Spitz."

Birrer then goes on to describe his system of training in which he "always saw to it that the dog went ahead of me when I held the leash .... If the dog led me so near a tree that I was in danger of hitting it I pulled the leash around the trunk until the dog felt some pain, in order to make him avoid trees, stones, etc. However, no one should think, regardless of what breed the dog is, that it can be trained only by being beaten; on the contrary, every trainer should make it his duty, when his animal has done well in his exercises, to pet him and make him a faithful friend, now and then giving him some delicacy to eat. It is only in this way that the dog will show his willingness and obedience to his master and will become attached and faithful."

In Britain, many other blind people of the ilk of Birrer and Reisinger were training, or using, dogs to act as their guides, judging by an exemption clause in a government statute over 100 years ago. The Customs and Inland Revenue Act of 1878, Section 21, Part three, which was an addendum to the instrument responsible for the introduction of dog licences in the United Kingdom, specifically absolved any blind person who used a dog as a guide from the necessity of taking out a licence for his charge.

Under the heading "Provision as to dogs used by blind persons", the statute states that "Nothing in the Dog Licences Act, 1867, or in this part of this Act, shall render a licence necessary in the case of a dog kept and used solely by a blind person for his or her guidance, or render such person liable to any penalty in respect of a dog so kept and used."

* * * *

The appalling number of casualties incurred as a result of the Great War included countless soldiers blinded on active service. The story goes that in an Oldenburg military hospital one Dr Gerhard Stalling left his shepherd dog in the care of a blind ex-soldier who was enjoying the sunshine in the infirmary gardens, whilst the physician went away to attend a meeting. When the doctor returned to collect his dog, he was so impressed (it is said) with the care and solicitousness with which the animal was attending upon the ex-serviceman, not to mention the creature's guiding capability as it walked along the garden path with the man following on the lead, that an idea blossomed in the physician's mind. Why not train dogs, in large numbers, to lead war-blinded veterans, and so enable ex-soldiers to return home at the earliest rather than languish forlornly in hospitals such as his?

Whilst this piquant tale adds an aura of romance to the advent of the modern, professionally-trained guide dog, and whilst it is patently true that the Germans played a great part in the instigation of the work, the development of training techniques would have a more mundane beginning. A beginning, in fact, which would stem from the writings of the like of Birrer, Reisinger, Courtney and Klein. Although these four blind gentlemen wrote only in an elementary manner about their exploits and methodology of training guide dogs, nevertheless their comments and practical application, in many instances, can be seen to have influenced the early 20th century German trainers and, indeed, persist to this day.

Stressing the benefits of his rudimentary harness and handle, Klein, for instance, says that the "use of a guiding stick has the advantage that the blind person notices at once when the dog is standing still, which is not true when he is led by a strap". Also, it is "grasped by the left hand of the blind person." The world over, guide dogs still are always trained to walk on the left of the blind person, with the obvious exception of amputees whose right arm might be the only usable upper limb.

Birrer has pertinent comments to make about obstacles under which a dog can proceed but a person might not: "The dog can be made attentive to the shafts on carriages, wagons, etc.; but the blind person must know precisely where these shafts may be since they are commonly chest high. If the dog does not pay attention to the height of these objects, which is difficult for him to do, one ought to pull him up by the leash and punish him until he has an idea of what is wanted." Birrer thus perceives the problem the dog may have in appreciating overhead obstacles which constitute a danger to the handler.

Reisinger's dogs too, were "careful never to go under partially lowered gates which would have bumped the master." And, "Walking always in front of his master the dog was always alert." The present-day guide dog must also always be alert insofar as good concentration on the work is concerned, and not being distracted by outside influences. The modern guide dog does not walk strictly in front of the handler, however. True, the animal forges a little ahead of the accompanying person, but keeps to the left whilst its hindquarters remain parallel to the handler's legs.

With so many blinded ex-servicemen anxious to become independent and mobile again, and since the books of Klein, Reisinger and Birrer would be printed in German, and standard works in the libraries of blind institutes, a perusal of these volumes would doubtless have encouraged the doctors and para-medical attendants of the day to turn their thoughts to guide dogs. By utilizing these animals, it might well facilitate rehabilitation of their blind patients and encourage self-help and independence and subsequent discharge from hospital.

Being in a military hospital, staffed by army doctors and nurses the medical people would naturally turn to dog trainers in the Armed Services to develop in a practical way their ideas regarding rehabilitation, through mobility, for their blind patients. To substantiate their thoughts on guide dogs for the blind, the relevant books by Birrer and others would be drawn to the attention of the trainers. It would not be too difficult for experienced and adaptable handlers of military dogs to turn their talents to endeavouring to supply blind ex-servicemen with guide dogs, particularly with printed instructions, albeit rudimentary and scanty, at their disposal.

As we will discuss later, not all blind people are suitable for guide dogs, and no doubt the military-cum-guide dog trainers of circa 1918 met with a modicum of failures in their efforts to train man and canine together as a working guide dog unit; but, on the other side of the coin, their success rate ran high. This success rate could in part be accounted for by the fact that the blind students with whom they would be working were, except for their visual handicap, fit, healthy, resolute and highly motivated young men who were anxious to become mobile and independent again.

Organised guide dog training by sighted professionals was thus an attempt to provide an answer to the rehabilitation, mobility and self-dependence needs of the extraordinary number of blinded ex-servicemen resulting from the calamitous conditions of the Great War. Whilst German military dog trainers made the transition to guide dog trainers with - perhaps - more zeal than skill, they were nevertheless firmly laying the foundations for the present-day sophisticated levels of both canine and human performance in this specialised field of mobility.

*   *   *   *

A 1935 booklet publicising an American organisation called the Eye Dog Movement for the Blind, and written by W.A.Christensen, himself one of the first guide dog owners in the United States, bears an illustration which makes a bold claim. The photograph is captioned "*Rolf* - the first dog ever trained to lead the blind." It portrays a Herr Kreimer, *Rolf* (an unidentified and unidentifiable breed of dog, probably cross-bred) and an un-named blind man: "A trio that made history in dogdom and brought hope to the blind", to quote Christensen.

Mr Christensen tells us that Lambert Kreimer was an officer in the Kaiser's bodyguard. Sent to the front, he was wounded and taken to a military hospital. Whilst there, he met up with a number of the 2,800 German soldiers blinded in the Great War. "Their greatest suffering", he remarked, "was caused by their inability to get about alone".

Kreimer considered a notion which had come to him. He had formerly trained circus, hunting and police dogs, so why couldn't he train dogs to lead the blind? When recovered from his wounds, he set about training a dog to do just that. The story goes that this dog was matched with a young blind veteran and Kreimer trained the two together over a period of 30 days. Once this stint of training was accomplished, the new man and dog team gave a demonstration of their mobility skills and safe travel to other blind ex-servicemen - whose interest was immediately aroused - and their sighted escorts, who were vividly describing the scene to them.

Having proved to the German authorities that guide dog training for the benefit of blind ex-soldiers on a grand scale was feasible, a school was established in Munich in 1919 under the direction of Kreimer. Three other schools were subsequently opened and within the space of 10 years 2,000 of Germany's war blind had been trained with guide dogs. All of these schools were, however, preceded by the guide dog training facility in the northern German town of Oldenburg initiated by Dr Stalling in 1916.

Mr John L. Sinykin, of Minneapolis, a breeder of German shepherd dogs, heard about the spread of guide dog training in Europe (there were also schools in France) and, not without difficulty, procured two trained dogs whilst he was visiting Germany and brought them back with him to the United States. One of Sinykin's greatest friends was a blind senator, Thomas D. Schall, also of Minneapolis, and it was to him that he assigned one of the two guide dogs in March 1926. Christensen, in his booklet, captions a photograph, "United States Senator Thomas D. Schall and *Lux,* the first eye dog imported to America". The second dog, *Eric,* another German shepherd, was placed with Colonel Fred Fitzpatrick, a blind war veteran and United States Marshal of Salina, Kansas. "I don't know what I would do without *Eric*", wrote the Colonel later, "I could not get along without him".

Sinykin himself matched Schall and Fitzpatrick with their dogs, and it was he who trained the two teams to work successfully together, simply through applying the scant knowledge gleaned by extremely limited observation of training methods during his relatively fleeting visit to Germany. No mean feat for a comparative novice, which reflected well upon the aptitude of his two students also.

Heartened by this advance, Sinykin established a training school for guide dogs at his La Salle kennels in Minneapolis and, again quoting Christensen, "is credited with having been the first man in America to realise this need of his fellow men who were blind and to take steps making it possible for more of them to have the companionship and guiding help of an eye dog".

Kreimer himself was induced to leave Germany and travel to the United States to help Sinykin get his project off the ground. It was then that Christensen procured one of the dogs Kreimer brought with him, *Almo*, a German shepherd, and the two were trained, in Los Angeles, to work exceedingly well together.

* * * *

Although the first guide dog training schools in Germany were geared to the needs of blinded ex-servicemen, the movement spread, quite rightly, to include civilian visually impaired citizens. In 1923 the "Guide Dog Organisation for German Civilian Blind" was established in Potsdam, near Berlin, under the leadership of trainers Ruecker and Wecherling. At about the same time, a wealthy American lady from Philadelphia, Mrs Dorothy Harrison Eustis, and her husband George, were in the process of establishing and developing "Fortunate Fields" in Vevey, Switzerland, a breeding and training establishment for German shepherd dogs, a breed in which she was passionately interested. "Fortunate Fields" dogs were trained in many avenues of ability, mainly pertaining to police and military work, and subsequently sold to a number of European government agencies who were becoming increasingly convinced of their worth as a useful adjunct to law and order.

Early in 1927 Mrs Eustis visited the guide dog school in Potsdam. She was profoundly impressed by what she saw and wrote in glowing terms an article called "The Seeing Eye", which was published in the "Saturday Evening Post" of 5th November, 1927. This article was brought to the attention of Morris Frank, a young blind man living in Nashville, Tennessee, which prompted him to write to Mrs Eustis asking her if she could provide him with a guide dog.

George Eustis and Jack Humphrey (a fellow American dog trainer at "Fortunate Fields") began the task of preparing a guide dog for Morris Frank. Their expertise was limited to comparatively brief but close observation of methods at Potsdam, and their own knowledge and application of dog training techniques generally. That they were successful in training Morris Frank with *Buddy*, a German shepherd dog, in Vevey in April, 1928, speaks highly of their joint efforts. These efforts were vindicated when Frank returned to America to work safely and well with Buddy for many years, thus publicly emphasising the value of such dogs as guides for blind people.

Hearing of Frank's exploits, a number of other blind people wrote to him expressing interest in getting a guide dog. Frank, in his turn, wrote to Mrs Eustis. Could she not continue her work of training guide dogs in America as well as in Switzerland, he asked? This approach led to the training of a small number of blind people with guide dogs in Nashville under the direction of Jack Humphrey, who had beforehand prepared the animals in Europe.

The generosity of a German shepherd dog breeder and trainer, Willi Ebeling, helped encourage the formative Seeing Eye organisation to move to Morristown in New Jersey. Here, The Seeing Eye, Inc., has remained since 1929, where they have produced countless guide dog units which have proved, and continue to prove, their worth all over the continent of America. Premises for the school were at first provided by Willi Ebeling, but in October 1931 Mrs Eustis helped purchase their present home, a large, beautiful country property at Whippany on the outskirts of Morristown. This is now one of the biggest and most sophisticated guide dog schools extant.

Between 1929 and 1931, Mrs Eustis established in Switzerland a training school for guide dog instructors called *l'Oeil qui Voit* (the Seeing Eye) which flourished for a little while, but became defunct when she devoted her interests to the infant organisation of the same name in Morristown.

Some astute trainers of differing nationalities were to learn their trade at *l'Oeil qui Voit*; three of them in those early days practised their craft in Britain. One was to remain as the first permanent trainer to the embryonic British guide dog movement. This stemmed from the initial enthusiasm of Mrs Rosamund Bond, a breeder of German shepherds, and Miss Muriel Crooke, another breed fancier, of Wallasey, in the county of Merseyside. They had heard of Mrs Eustis's exploits and written to her in the hope of setting up a guide dog organisation in Britain. On 23rd September 1930 the three ladies met in London to discuss their ideas. Mrs Eustis said she would lend the Guide Dog Committee (two new supporters, Lady Kitty Ritson and Captain Alan Sington had joined Miss Crooke and Mrs Bond to help them in their efforts) a trainer to instigate an experimental scheme in Britain.

The temporary trainer, William Debetaz, accompanied by Jack Humphrey, duly arrived in Wallasey in July 1931 and selected seven German shepherd bitches from 28 animals which had been offered for training to the organisation from various sources. Humphrey returned to Switzerland whilst Debetaz (who later joined The Seeing Eye, Inc., in Morristown) took the seven potential guide dogs under his wing. In October 1931 the first class of four blind students assembled in Wallasey. A few months later warm words of praise were to emanate from the successful quartet.

"My dog has given me glorious freedom and independence," said Allen Caldwell. Fellow student Musgrave Frankland eulogised, "A guide dog is almost equal in many ways to giving a blind man sight itself." The other two students, Thomas Ap Rhys and George Lamb, were equally as enthusiastic.

Two further classes were held in England under the direction of an Italian instructor, G. A. Gabriel, before it was decided that a permanent trainer was now a necessity. Captain Nicolai Liakhoff was recommended for the post by Mrs Eustis. A former officer in the Russian Imperial Guard, Liakhoff landed in England in October, 1933, since when the Guide Dogs for the Blind Association (the title adopted in October, 1934, and by which it has been known ever since) has gone from strength to strength. A newspaper reporter wrote of Liakhoff, "By a rare blend of faith, knowledge and fortitude, he has brought the guide dog movement in Britain to an impressive pitch of development".

Such developments were not being confined to the British Isles; since those early days guide dog training centres have been established in many other parts of the world. In the United States, an impressive number of nationwide schools have become well-known names besides that of The Seeing Eye., Inc., and centres are now firmly established in, among other countries, Australia, New Zealand, South Africa, Canada, Holland, Belgium, Norway, France, Italy, Japan, Germany and Eire.

The Wallasey establishment was closed during the second World War, and guide dog operations moved to a larger and more fitting centre in Leamington Spa. Nicolai Liakhoff, sadly, is no longer with us. Even he would have been astonished at the support commanded by, and the formidable strength of, the Guide Dogs for the Blind Association of the present day. Financial security, a large staff, a total annual output of about 800 guide dog units, a head office in Berkshire, a puppy breeding and rearing centre at Warwick, and eight regionally based training schools, together with a number of smaller ancillary establishments, as well as an involvement with wider aspects of blind mobility and welfare, all bear testimony to the dedication and industry of Captain Nicolai Liakhoff, and to the conviction and foresight of an American lady called Dorothy Harrison Eustis.

2

PSYCHOLOGICAL ASPECTS

"Humans differ from animals in that humans are capable of reflective thought, i.e., humans are able to manipulate symbols in such a manner as to act upon themselves (self as object), whereas animals are incapable of complex symbolic thought and respond merely to stimuli on the basis of conditioned responses or innate reflex action."

Ben H. Knott

How can dogs be trained to perform particular actions?

How do animals learn? Indeed, what is learning? As far as animal behaviour is concerned we define learning as the process which encourages change in individual conduct as a consequence of experience.

The five evident types of learning which present themselves are: *Habituation*, which is a never-ending progression of accommodation and adaptation to suit a particular environment. Pre-existing responses wane (alarm at a loud noise; cringing away at the sight of a passing lorry) when repeated stimulation fails to be followed by reward or punishment. *Conditioning*, the formation of a reflex action, a response, brought about through habit or training, to a stimulus not normally connected with it. For example, the guide dog stops (conditioned response) at the down-kerb (stimulus), but this action has only been acquired through prior conditioning by the trainer.

The three further forms of learning bear less relevance to guide dog training, but nevertheless might impinge upon certain aspects of it. *Trial-and-Error* learning occurs where repeated endeavours, by haphazardly employing random responses, attains the desired goal when one of these unrelated actions meets with success. In repeated trials this successful movement comes earlier and earlier until ultimately it is given as soon as the situation presents itself. *Latent Learning* is a simple acquisition of knowledge not demonstrated by specific behaviour at the time of the experience. Such learning is effected without reward. The orientating ability of some animals might be an example of Latent Learning. The lost dog finding its way home, for instance, because of a knowledge of landmarks and streets gained latently. *Insight* is learning through mental discernment, usually by a sudden understanding of the solution to a problem. This sort of learning is invariably restricted to *Homo Sapiens* although some evidence has been produced to indicate that, in isolated instances, chimpanzees have solved simple problems through flashes of insight.

Behaviour which is positively reinforced persists and is strengthened; behaviour which is negatively reinforced diminishes and dies. This is the basis of operant conditioning. A dog does something that the owner wants it to do, and he praises it for doing so. The words of approbation are a reward, a positive reinforcer, and in this way the dog is encouraged to repeat the action on another occasion.

The dog does something which the owner does not want it to do, and it is scolded, perhaps physically punished, for so doing. This punishment, this negative reinforcer, discourages the dog from repeating the deed on a subsequent opportunity.

To facilitate learning, to have the dog perform well, or desist from bad behaviour, these positive and negative reinforcers must be applied almost simultaneously alongside the proper (or improper) conduct to attain the desired effect. After a particular fitting, or unfitting, action, the longer the lapse of time before praise or punishment, the slower will the dog be to learn.

Therefore, if the dog is required to sit, and it does so, the animal is praised at the point where it has completed the desired action, not a few moments later. If this lapse in time is allowed before telling the dog how good it is, the animal will not associate the reward (words of praise) with the deed (sitting) and conditioning does not take place as effectively as it should. Similarly, if the dog is sniffing at a lamp-post, the moment to correct it, to fleetingly punish it, both by a sharp jerk on the lead and admonitory words, is at that precise instant when it is smelling the scent on the standard. It would be futile to attempt to negatively reinforce this undesirable behaviour either before the event takes place (on the other hand, precipitate action on the part of the trainer can prevent the dog from sniffing in the first place, which is preferable to correcting the misconduct when it occurs) or after the animal has stopped being wayward.

The concepts of positive reinforcement and negative reinforcement are all important, and a third and vital element in conditioning is that component known as the stimulus.

To effect operant behaviour a stimulus may not always be present, but as we shall see later, it plays a crucial part in the conditioning of the guide dog. We here must differentiate between classical conditioning and operant conditioning.

Classical conditioning is a process whereby a response comes to be evoked by a stimulus other than that to which it is the natural reaction. The term came to be used to describe that phenomena where a reflex, naturally following on a stimulus, progresses to being elicited by a different stimulus through the constant association of the two stimuli together.

The name of Ivan Petrovich Pavlov, the Russian physiologist born in 1849, is synonymous with the concept of classical conditioning. While observing the behaviour of dogs in his laboratory, Pavlov noticed that the sight of food, let alone the taste of it, was enough to promote salivation. The dogs' salivary responses to the introduction of food into the mouth Pavlov considered to be the unconditioned reflex, an innate, uncontrolled reaction, whilst when the animals salivated to the sight of food, this was a learned response; a conditioned reflex.

By associating food with the ticking of a metronome, the ringing of a bell, or (visually) the rotation of a disc, Pavlov found that the dogs responded appropriately by salivating. A repetition of the various stimuli (metronome, bell, disc) soon had the animals salivating to the sounds or sights alone.

The dog in Pavlov's laboratory had, through a process of simple conditioning, learnt to salivate in anticipation of being fed. Originally, the food (unconditioned stimulus) had needed to be taken into the mouth before salivation (unconditioned response) took place, but now the sound of a bell (conditioned stimulus), having previously been paired with the food to initiate learning, was alone sufficient to evoke salivation, which was now therefore considered to be a conditioned response. (Figure 2-1).

Elaborating on his discoveries Pavlov found that reversing the procedure of association without offering a reward led to extinction, preceded by fading, (Figure 2-2) of the conditioned response. That is to say, if the bell sounded and food was not thereafter offered, before long the response was extinguished. However, conditioned responses, once acquired, are most persistent, and a re-introduction of the conditioning technique soon leads to recovery of the appropriate response. In fact, spontaneous recovery (figure 2-3) results in a heightened response upon resumption of extinction trials.

Figure 2-1

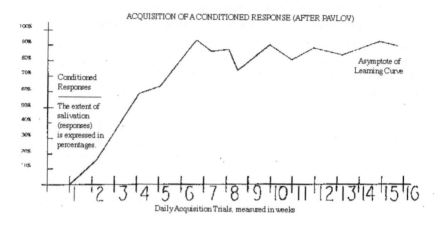

ACQUISITION OF A CONDITIONED RESPONSE (AFTER PAVLOV)

Conditioned Responses

The extent of salivation (responses) is expressed in percentages.

Asymptote of Learning Curve

Daily Acquisition Trials, measured in weeks

Figure 2-2

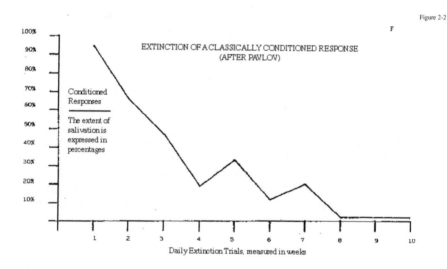

EXTINCTION OF A CLASSICALLY CONDITIONED RESPONSE (AFTER PAVLOV)

Conditioned Responses

The extent of salivation is expressed in percentages

Daily Extinction Trials, measured in weeks

28

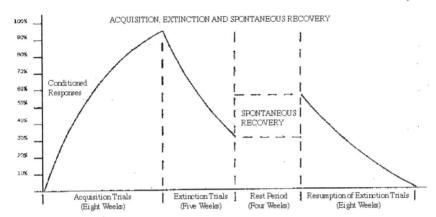

Figure 2-3

ACQUISITION, EXTINCTION AND SPONTANEOUS RECOVERY

The theories pertaining to animal learning thus owe much to the endeavour and perseverance of Pavlov. The basis of nomenclature of the conditioning process might also be ascribed to him. Yet it is the American psychologist B. F. Skinner who springs to the forefront as far as the theoretical aspects of guide dog training are concerned. Not that Skinner was concerned with guide dog training. His researches were into animal learning generally. But the outcome of his experiments prove relevant to understanding the rudiments upon which guide dog training is formulated.

Previous to the advent of Skinner, however, another American, Edward L. Thorndike (1874-1949) also evaluated a stimulus – response relationship as a fundamental for understanding animal learning when he studied a cat confined to a cage with a morsel of food planted outside and a way of escape - a loop of string to pull aside a bolt - within reach. Random movements on the part of the cat eventually led to the string being unintentionally pulled and the hatch opened, releasing the cat to eat the food. With repeated trials, this successful outcome to the cat's exploits became increasingly frequent. The stimulus of the string led to the conditioned response of pulling it with the reward of food as the positive reinforcer.

Thorndike postulated that animals adopt correct courses of action neither by reasoning or instinct, but by the gradual learning of the appropriate response. His findings he called the *law of effect*: this law of learning stated that stimulus - response situations depended not only on the stimulus and response occurring together, but also on the effects that followed the response. Thorndike differentiated these effects as *satisfiers* and *annoyers*, thus determining whether or not subsequent responses would be

29

strengthened or weakened. Animal behaviourists would now describe Thorndike's satisfiers as positive reinforcers, and annoyers as negative reinforcers.

Thorndike's conclusions with cats were taking place in the 1890's, whilst almost at the same time a British psychologist, C. Lloyd Morgan, was postulating that animal actions which appeared to be the result of thought processes could be explained by 'trial and error' learning.

Morgan observed: "The way in which my dog learnt to lift the latch of the garden gate, and thus let himself out, affords a good example of trial-and-error learning .... When my fox terrier was put outside the door, he naturally wanted to get onto the road, where there was much to tempt him - the chance to run, other dogs to sniff at, possibly cats to be worried. He gazed out through the railings and in due time happened to be under the latch, lifting it with his head. He then withdrew and looked elsewhere, but meanwhile the gate swung open. Here was a *fortunate occurrence* arising out of the natural tendencies in a dog.... After some 10 or 12 similar experiences, in each of which the exit was more rapidly effected with less and less gazing out at wrong places, the fox terrier learnt to go straight to the right spot. In this case the lifting of the latch was unquestionably hit on by accident, and the trick was only rendered habitual by the associations of the chance act and the happy escape....No logical thinking on the dog's part is necessary for the interpretation of the facts, and we should not assume its presence since the evidence does not compel us to do so". This proposition led to the formulation of an axiom that still holds good in psychological research, and is known as *Lloyd Morgan's Canon*, viz., explication of animal behaviour must be at the lowest level consistent with observation.

*   *   *   *

Burrhus F. Skinner was born in 1904. He identified two categories of simple learning. Firstly, there is respondent conditioning (which is Pavlov's classical conditioning) where, given the requisite stimulus, the response occurs automatically. In Pavlovian conditioning, however, we must first of all have an unconditioned stimulus on which to base learning. Additionally, the stimulus itself proves to be the reinforcer (in Pavlov's experiments, for instance, the salivation response is rewarded by the presentation of the food, which is, of course, the unconditioned stimulus, but now becomes the reinforcer) and such learning only takes place at a reflexive level via the autonomic nervous system.

The second category of conditioning is recognised as very much the brainchild of Skinner. Operant conditioning, as opposed to the autonomic level of classical conditioning, functions through voluntary modes of action and behaviour. Skinner places greater emphasis upon the response and reinforcement aspects of learning, and less on the stimuli; Pavlov's postulations were more concerned with the stimulus and the response, and these on a lower level of learning than that of Skinner, Morgan and Thorndike.

A guide dog, once conditioned to a stimulus - response situation which brings a reward, will endeavour to repeat the action on subsequent occasions. Similarly, if a stimulus - response situation brings punishment and pain, avoidance will ensue. In as many words, we are here describing Thorndike's law of effect, which, but for refinement, is akin to Skinner's hypothesis relating to operant conditioning. Thorndike was a pioneer in experimental animal psychology. After formulating his law of effect, he later placed more emphasis on the nature of reward in the strengthening of connections (between stimulus and response) and felt that negative reinforcement might not always produce enduring defects. That is to say, positive reinforcement has more impact than negative reinforcement. It is better to reward than punish if learning is to be facilitated. Which is the very point that Skinner amplifies in relation to operant conditioning.

Operant behaviour is described as conditioning, but there is a wide gulf between it and the classical conditioning of reflexes as shown by Pavlov. Operant conditioning is a more sophisticated process than the voluntary learning as defined by Thorndike. If an operant response (e.g., stopping at the down-kerb) occurs and is followed by positive reinforcement ("Good dog") then the probability of such action recurring is increased.

As we shall see later, guide dog training operates on a considerably higher plane than classical conditioning as perfected by Pavlov who, incidentally, was observing the physiological peculiarities of learning rather than the psychological. Thorndike and Skinner looked at learning from the purely behavioural standpoint. The basis of such learning follows a stimulus - response - reinforcement pattern which in practice is the model for guide dog training. As an example, the guide dog arrives at the down-kerb (stimulus) and stops (response) and the handler says warmly "Good dog" (reinforcement). Similarly, the animal comes across a compelling aroma (stimulus) on a lamp-post and sniffs it (response), but the handler jerks the lead severely and says with feeling "Bad dog" (reinforcement). These two simple practical examples serve to illustrate the words of Jeremy Bentham (1748-1832), the British philosopher who said that we do all those things that give us pleasure, and avoid those that give us pain. This we know as the *doctrine of hedonism* - that every act is motivated by a desire for pleasantness or by an aversion to unpleasantness. No animal is more dedicated to this doctrine than the dog.

31

Regarding the autonomous reflexes in the dog as experimented on by Pavlov, it is the unconditioned stimulus which is the reinforcer, whereas in operant conditioning the reinforcer is the reward (or, in Thorndike's terminology, the satisfier). When we discuss the practical training of guide dogs, and we note the voluntary responses of these canines in relation to the stimuli presented, and the subsequent appropriate reinforcement of their efforts by the trainer, the operant conditioning *modus operandi* of animal learning, *a la* Thorndike and Skinner, evidences itself as the simple formula stimulus - response - reinforcement unfolds.

Once a conditioned response to a specific stimulus has been learnt, must it thereafter always be reinforced? In actual fact, schedules of reinforcement, when conditioning is complete, can be varied. Until a consistent and ready response is forthcoming, the most expeditious schedule is utilised, that is, *continuous reinforcement*, whereby every response is rewarded. Once a lesson is learnt, however, different schedules might be employed, notably *intermittent reinforcement*, which, as the name suggests is the application of reinforcement at varying intervals between responses. In other words, some responses are not reinforced; it is not necessary to say "Good dog" every time the animal stops at the down-kerb. Skinner, in fact, found that intermittent reinforcement was superior to continuous reinforcement (once the response was learnt) in maintaining a consistent response pattern.

Whichever schedule is adopted, the fact must be accepted that, now and then, a response will not be forthcoming albeit the conditioned stimulus is present. On occasion the dog, which has previously been conditioned to stopping at the down-kerb, without warning overshoots it. Why is this? The dog may have been inhibited externally; that is, its interest may have been fixed on a stray dog, or a cat nearby. A passer-by might even be cajoling the dog with tempting words or gestures. In the face of these distractions *external inhibition* may be so strong that the response to the stimulus of the kerb is forsaken.

A further factor to affect the requisite response might be *internal inhibition*. The beginnings of internal inhibition are evinced when a trained dog, having overshot the kerb, is not negatively reinforced at the moment it goes over the edge of the pavement, and brought back and re-positioned at the down-kerb where it is now positively reinforced (praised). If this is not done, then on subsequent occasions the dog may overshoot further kerbs. Brought to its logical conclusion this *fading* process will ultimately lead to *extinction* of the conditioned response. To overcome such a failing, the dog is corrected when it overshoots the kerb, but it is praised when it is returned to the pavement edge. This is most important; the down-kerb must always be a pleasant place for the dog to be at. Negative reinforcement would only serve to discourage the dog from stopping at or near the kerb edge.

The change of hand which takes place when the dog is allocated to the blind person can also lead to some measure of internal inhibition. For conditioned responses to be consistently forthcoming, the circumstances of enactment must be constant. Any change, no matter how minor, of, for instance, relationships or surroundings, can lead to internal inhibition. So it is that when the blind person first begins handling his new guide dog, a certain amount of internal inhibition can be expected. Appropriate negative and positive reinforcement on the part of the new handler, under the direction, initially, of the trainer, to counteract inhibited responses will, in a comparatively short space of time, put matters right.

All of this adds to the difficulties faced by the blind person training with a new guide dog, which even where conditioned responses are forthcoming at maximum intensity can be fraught enough. Thanks to the resilience of the novice owner, aided and supported by the trainer who renders assistance where need be, it is not too long before the balance is redressed, and the guide dog has adapted to suit the new situation under the jurisdiction of a different handler, so that conditioned responses are forthcoming as they should. Without amelioration during training of blind person and guide dog together, inhibited conditioned responses may well become, sadly, a permanent feature of performance.

The change of environment facing the animal when the guide dog accompanies its new master to the home surroundings introduces further frustration through inhibited responses, but again the resourcefulness of the blind person, together with the application of dog handling skills as previously taught - albeit this time perhaps without the helping hand of the trainer-resolves the position.

* * * *

Two phenomena occurring in conditioning and of importance to guide dog training are *generalisation* and *discrimination*. Dependent upon the stimuli presented to the trained guide dog, and dependent upon the situation in which the animal finds itself, it will be expected to display capabilities of generalising or discriminating to suit the circumstances.

For instance, the dog is trained to stop at the down-kerb. Some kerbs are high, some are low; some are rounded, some are square; some face across wide, busy roads, some across narrow, insignificant alley-ways. But, where-ever there is a pavement edge which fronts into a street or lane, no matter how slight the drop, the dog is expected to generalise to the extent that it must stop at all down-kerbs. If the dog begins to discriminate, and attempts to stop only at deep down-kerbs facing busy roads, suitable reinforcement applied by the trainer will encourage the animal to come to a halt at each and every pavement edge.

Conversely, in obstacle work, which we discuss in a later chapter, the guide dog is expected to discriminate between obstructions which necessitate leaving the pavement in order to avoid them, and those where it is possible to remain on the path. If a wide enough gap is evident between the obstruction and the building line, let us say, then it will be much safer and more expeditious to use this breach rather than go into the road to get round the obstruction. The dog must learn to generalise to the extent that it takes avoiding action for all obstacles, no matter how much they may differ in size and shape (ladders, public service barriers, open cellar holes, prams and bicycles across the pavement, and what have you), and it must learn to be discriminating enough to use the pedestrian paths (where width allows) between obstructions when these present themselves.

During initial obstacle training, it may be found that the dog will generalise and endeavour to step into the roadway to go round all obstructions on the pavement, but as time goes on, with appropriate reinforcement, the animal learns to discriminate between those obstacles which must be negotiated by going into the road, and those barriers which can be dealt with whilst remaining on the path.

Traffic training (to be discussed in more detail later) provides an example of the possible dangers of discrimination. Traffic work initially necessitates the use of a car belonging to the training agency, and driven by a co-worker. The dog is conditioned to ignore the command "Forward" to cross the road should a moving car be close by. To begin with, the dog is presented with the agency vehicle, and it is not too long before, with fitting reinforcement, the refusal of the injunction to move off becomes evident and the animal crosses the road only when the car has passed by.

However, it is found, especially during the early days of traffic training, that the dog discriminates and stops only for the agency car and is prepared to ignore other vehicles, even when in a position of some danger. This provides an example of discrimination which is decidedly undesirable as far as guide dog training is concerned. Fortunately, it is not at all difficult, as we shall see later, to stamp out such discrimination and to have the dog generalising, as it should, in relation to traffic work.

Although there may be individual differences in each dog's capacity and readiness to absorb learning, these will not be great. The practical application of the trainer, together with his ability and diligence, will hold greater sway on the rate of canine learning, but an important consideration is the motivation of the dog. A major motive, as was mentioned earlier, is the doctrine of hedonism, which the dog follows slavishly.

What additional form might motivation take to encourage the dog to readily submit to conditioning so that desired responses are elicited via various stimuli? It is the motivation of the dog to be responsive to the wishes of its superior. The dog is a pack animal. In the wild state it was accustomed to obeying the dictates of the pack-leader. It knew its place in the social order of the pack, and if it went beyond those bounds, the pack-leader would soon forcibly bring it to heel. As a domesticated animal the dog looks upon (or should look upon) its owner, or trainer, or handler, as the pack-leader. In the eyes of the dog, the human being is also a dog, but a most superior sort of dog. And the wishes of the human pack-leader must be respected and obeyed, just as they would be in the wild state. If, however, the owner is not prepared, or is ill-equipped, to substantiate his position of authority, the dog will take advantage of its master's weakness and disobey injunctions whenever the mood takes it. This unfortunate state of affairs will continue for as long as the owner is unable or unwilling to assume power, and to reinforce stringently all commands to which the dog had previously failed to respond.

3

Puppy - Walking

When does training a guide dog start, and when does it finish? If we consider training to be the total socialisation, conditioning and habituation of the animal, then it starts almost from birth. Even as the puppy first emerges into the world it is becoming habituated to the environment in which it now lives. A little later it is taken in hand by its human master and is socialised (or should be) to the extent that it might become acceptable not only to the immediate family of which it is a part, but also to the world at large. It does not mess in the house; it does not jump up at people; it lies quietly under a table when in a restaurant; it trots quietly alongside when master is shopping; it does not beg for food; it does not bite people; it does not chase other animals; all this and more is part of the socialisation process so that the dog becomes a better individual to live with and have around the house and take on excursions.

As the puppy matures, as it grows and develops, so it becomes ever more well socialised and an object of good behaviour. Interwoven with this process of socialisation is that of conditioning. The animal is conditioned to respond to the command "Sit" and all other injunctions one expects a good dog to obey promptly. It is conditioned - in the case of a guide dog - to walk, free of distraction, at the left hand side of its handler, slightly ahead, maintaining steady pressure but not pulling on the lead, with its hindquarters alongside its master's left leg and not deviating needlessly from a straight course.

For this transitional advance of socialisation, habituation and conditioning to take place, and in order for the process to be adequate enough for the guide dog to take its position in society, it will be obvious that the puppy must be reared in home surroundings rather than whiling its time away within the non-stimulating environment of the kennel. But because the demand for guide dogs is so great, and because output of trained animals from each training centre is correspondingly large, there are therefore many more puppies than can possibly be individually dealt with at the school itself, which is why the guide dog agencies are glad to avail themselves of the services of puppy-walkers. Indeed, without such services the output of guide dogs would be severely curtailed.

Puppy-walkers come from all sorts of families and from all walks of life. Ideally, they should live in urban surroundings and have one or more children, besides a pet or two, preferably a cat and perhaps a canary, budgie or rabbit. In this way the puppy, living as one of the family, becomes accustomed and friendly towards children, cats and other animals whilst it is becoming habituated to the hubbub of the everyday urban environment.

A puppy-walker is a man, woman or responsible adolescent who takes an eight-week old embryonic guide dog into his home as part of the family until it is about 12-months old, at which age it goes to the training centre for testing and assessment. All being well, guide dog training proper is then instigated for a period of five months, upon which the animal is matched to a suitable blind person and the two are trained together. At the end of a three to four week training stint the man and his new guide dog, now functioning in unison as a team, return home to begin a fresh life together as a working partnership.

From this continuum of events the importance of the puppy-walking sequence is evident. Without it, the chain would be broken and a substitute link would most likely be inadequate to meet the demands of socialisation, habituation and conditioning. In other words, the quality of the finished unit of blind person with guide dog would be adversely affected. Willing and conscientious puppy-walkers are people therefore very much welcomed by the various guide dog training organisations.

Although it might appear that the demands made upon puppy-walkers are great, in actual fact the guide dog agency asks no more than that the puppy is reared indoors as part of the family, that it be house-trained and sociable to other people and animals, and that it is taught to walk properly on the lead and becomes inured to a hectic urban environment. As a bonus, however, it is useful if the dog is disciplined to behaving impeccably indoors - to go to its bed when instructed, to lie uncomplainingly there, or elsewhere in the room, when family and friends are meeting or dining together. To remain indoors, alone, for increasingly lengthier periods whilst the family is out. Not to pester callers who are invited into the house. And to respond to a growing number of commands as time goes on. To understand and respond to verbal correction, and when it does well, to indicate contentment at warm words of praise.

Out-of-doors the puppy will be encouraged to walk on the left and slightly ahead of the handler, with some tension on the lead, and not to stop and sniff or be interested overmuch in other dogs, or people passing by. Of course, initially the very young puppy will be allowed to satisfy its natural curiosity, and to meet other animals in an equable way, and to explore a new environment until its inquisitiveness is satisfied. As the weeks go by, however, the puppy will be expected to keep to a direct path along the pavement as it proceeds along its way, and if it shows any inclination to be distracted, the puppy-walker will check it and not allow its attention to be diverted.

When the puppy is six months old, attendance at a local training club can be useful to consolidate commands such as "Sit", "Down", "Stay", and "Come". Walking to heel, however, is not recommended since the guide dog, when working, must always be a little ahead of the handler. In parks and fields, when the dog is allowed to run free, emphasis is laid upon a prompt response to the command "Come". A ready recall by a puppy to its handler is an important pre-requisite for guide dog training.

Animals farmed out for puppy-walking are from approved stock which, in the past, has proved successful. The dog is delivered to the puppy-walker complete with collar, lead, grooming brush and comb, and dog bed. The puppy has been checked to be worm free, and examined by a veterinary surgeon to ascertain good health. During development, the puppy will of course be inoculated against hard pad, distemper, hepatitis, leptospira and parvovirus. All veterinary treatment is paid for by the parent guide dog organisation, as are the feeding expenses.

The progress of the dog is periodically monitored by the puppy-walking supervisor, and any faults in the animal which give cause for concern are, where possible, corrected. In extreme instances, such as persistent aggressive tendencies, or uncontrollable fear of environmental features, the dog may be withdrawn and subsequently rejected. Such instances are, happily, rare. In fact, 85 per cent of puppy-walked animals eventually graduate as successful guide dogs.

The puppy is kept to a nourishing diet, again acting on the advice of the supervising guide dog agency, and food between meals, eating titbits and accepting morsels from friends and strangers alike is totally discouraged, as are any scavenging tendencies whether on or off the lead. The feeding of fish or fowl bones is frowned upon, also white bread; and food or liquids straight from the fridge is not particularly encouraged.

As a wholesome diet, with intervals of four hours between, the young puppy might have, for breakfast, brown bread, biscuit, cereal or groats, with milk and, perhaps, a raw egg added. Lunch would comprise raw meat chopped into small pieces. As an alternative to meat, cooked fish (no bones) could be fed, with brown bread or biscuit meal. At mid-afternoon, repeat as for breakfast, and supper is a duplication of lunch.

Proprietary puppy foods can be used as alternatives to some of the meals, and fresh water should always be available. Bonemeal and cod liver oil are useful, indeed necessary, additions to the puppy's diet.

The number of meals diminishes as the puppy grows older, until, when mature, one feed a day is given. This will basically consist of tinned meat (or a proprietary brand of dehydrated food) together with biscuit and chopped vegetable. The amount dependent upon the dog's breed and size. Time of day for feeding is arbitrary, although usually lunchtime or early evening.

* * * *

When the young animal first arrives at the puppy-walker's house it is allowed to explore its new surroundings, and will need some measure of reassurance from its guardian as it begins to adjust to its fresh way of life. Over-protection of the puppy by the walker is, however, discouraged. After all, the dog must grow up as an animal of some mettle. The puppy is shown its own particular bed in some inconspicuous corner of the house, and is encouraged to go there, to the accompaniment of the word of command "Bed" whenever it shows signs of tiredness or, indeed, when the walker wishes not to have the animal under his feet. All this, of course, takes place over a period of time, until such occasion when the dog responds promptly to "Bed" and stays there, even when the family is out of the house, and until such time as the puppy-walker deems that the dog may leave its basket. If the older puppy desists from remaining in its bed, or makes a noise whilst staying there, it is propelled back to the basket and clipped rudely on the nose with the flat of the hand as it is told sternly to "Stay".

But long before this, when the puppy is still very much a baby, compelling it to stay in its bed will only be for short periods of time. More essential at this early stage will be house training. So first thing in the morning and last thing at night, after every meal, after a daytime nap, and after playtime with the children or another animal, the puppy is allowed outside to do the necessary, upon which occasion it is lavishly praised. It is useful to associate the word "Busy" with the act, since this will encourage the dog, later on, to do as is bidden readily.

It should not be too long before the puppy cottons on to what is required, but to help it control its bladder, liquid intake should be monitored and curtailed somewhat after six o'clock in the evening, until such is its stage of development that the dog is able to restrain itself indoors for longer periods. If an accident does happen, scold the dog roundly, indicating the site of its misdemeanour, and then take the puppy immediately out-of-doors so that it begins to appreciate whereabouts it should relieve itself as opposed to the Persian carpet.

When the puppy eventually qualifies as a guide dog, it is obviously advantageous if it does not relieve itself whilst working in harness, in the company of the blind owner. Therefore, before setting out on a walk with the puppy on a lead, the walker should encourage the dog to do its business in an overgrown spot in the garden or elsewhere. If, however, during the walk the puppy wishes to relieve itself, it should be quickly compelled to go into the gutter to do so. Hopefully, with practice and routine, the animal will understand the necessity for attending the overgrown patch in the garden, and walks on the lead subsequently remain uninterrupted.

For the puppy to become used to collar and lead, and to walk correctly as befits a future guide dog, two jaunts a day along urban streets involving a multitude of environmental conditions are useful, but should be undertaken without tiring the little animal. Free exercise in park, field or garden is naturally enough not only beneficial to use up surplus energy, but useful to promote healthy growth of bone, muscle and tissue, as well as providing an opportunity to practice the recall when the puppy is running loose.

As the dog develops, the length of walk can be increased, and an infinite variety of situations might be contended with so that the animal remains steady and unworried no matter the circumstances in which it finds itself. On the lead, the dog must walk straight ahead in the centre of the pavement, and not be distracted. If it does pay attention to that which it should not, it is scolded verbally and encouraged to ignore such distractions by words of praise once it has responded to the vocal chastisement. It is not necessary, and indeed it is frowned upon, for the puppy-walker to teach the dog to sit at the kerb. This avenue of training will be judiciously introduced at a later stage. However, if it is impossible, because of the traffic flow, for the puppy-walker to cross an intersecting road, then on such an occasion the dog should be made to wait quietly with the handler at the down-kerb, until the vehicles have gone and it is clear to proceed in a straight line towards the opposite up-kerb.

When the very young puppy is first introduced to town conditions, the manner of its acceptance of this urban environment should be noted. Some puppies are naturally bold and find little to fear in these surroundings; other dogs, however, are a little more doubtful and will seek reassurance from the escort. The puppy-walker is asked to be sympathetic in the handling of the dog in his care, but more especially towards the latter type of unsure animal. A warm, comforting tone of voice from the handler will help the puppy retain its composure, and to let it know that there is nothing to fear from the strange sights and sounds which surround it. The puppy-walker should allow it a full rein of lead so that there is no undue restriction of movement when the dog begins to show doubt and apprehension at those environmental features which confront it. Nevertheless, the walker should most definitely endeavour to complete this particular route, perhaps past milling crowds, pneumatic drills, power compressors, schoolchildren pouring out of playgrounds, large dogs rushing up barking, heavy lorries rolling past, and all the clutter and impedimenta which comprises a town centre street, but in so doing the puppy is allowed the length of the lead within which it can explore its surroundings. The dog should not be dragged past offending objects. Where it shows uncertainty, the puppy may stand still whilst satisfying its curiosity at the source of doubt. It is permitted to approach and sniff the object (it might, for instance, be a heap of black plastic rubbish bags which is the cause of its discomfiture) and thus alleviate its apprehension before proceeding further on the walk.

With advancing weeks, as the small puppy grows both in stature and confidence, it will take all such former causes of consternation in its stride, and walks can proceed without interruption. The puppy-walker can now concentrate on having the dog walk at a steady and comfortable pace, free of distraction, in the correct position at the left side of the handler in the centre of the pavement. And by now it will be quite used to travelling on buses (where it will lie quietly under the seat), visiting shops and restaurants, going on railway stations and up steps and on lifts, over bridges and under subways, and it will not be disturbed by loud noises, heavy traffic on congested roads and throngs of pedestrians on the pavement. In short, it will be as completely habituated as it possibly can be to our modern, bustling, polluted and noisy world.

Additionally it will be responding promptly to the general obedience words of command. For instance, the injunction "Sit", upon which command the dog will have been trained to do so by the puppy-walker. The handler will effect this action when the animal, collar and lead affixed, is correctly positioned at his left. With lead in right hand, a short, sharp command "Sit" is issued as the handler pushes the dog's hindquarters to the ground. The front legs of the puppy must remain static, the hind legs bend, go forward and tuck under the animal as it sits facing squarely ahead without twisting or turning. The puppy-walker, too, faces ahead but, initially, keeps his left hand on the rump of the sitting dog in case it tries to get up again whilst the handler is praising it. It is wise not to be over eloquent with praise for this simple exercise, otherwise the dog may take this as a signal to alter position, turn towards the handler, and perhaps stand up again. Therefore, only a modicum of praise will suffice. Bearing this in mind, it should not be too long before the stimulus of the word of command "Sit" elicits the conditioned response; the handler should effect speed by re-introducing a sharp and ruthless push down on the hindquarters with the left hand if recalcitrance is evident. Having the dog sit, and additional aspects of general obedience are further dealt with in chapter six.

Frequent use of the puppy's name is to be encouraged, to further instant recognition and attention by the animal of its appellation, which is so crucial in all spheres of interaction between man and dog. Simply by changing the tone of voice whilst expressing the dog's name, dissatisfaction, discouragement, inspiration or pleasure, in fact a staggering range of feelings and implications, can be directed at, and appreciated by, the puppy.

By the time maturity is reached, the dog is responsive to all modulations of the human voice, and is totally composed within the framework of modern civilisation. Shortly, the young adult animal will be collected by the puppy-walking supervisor and taken to the training centre, ready to begin a new, progressive phase in its life with the introduction of guide dog work. The departure of the dog can prove rather a sad occasion for the puppy-walker, since both human and canine parties have, not unnaturally, developed some affinity and affection between them. However, as far as the walker is concerned, the parting is assuaged somewhat by the delivery of a new puppy to replace the dog now departing. That is, if a new puppy is requested. Perhaps the puppy-walker has decided that he will not take a replacement to care for, and accept the responsibility for fostering its development during its formative months. Whether a superseding animal is taken or not, the puppy-walker can look back with no little satisfaction on the significant part he has played in the fashioning of a future guide dog and companion.

4

TEMPERAMENT

The natural disposition, the temperament, of the dog is of crucial importance when deciding upon its suitability for training as a guide. Without an optimum balance of most temperamental traits, notwithstanding the fact that such an animal could possibly be trained, a canine's performance as a guide dog would suffer.

Charting the temperament of the dog is considerably less complicated than attempting to explain the disposition of emotionally bound man. Yet both human and canine traits of character are partially inherited and partly influenced by the environment, and by those significant others with whom we live and, in the wider world, individuals we come into contact with. We have already discussed the importance of such socialisation as far as the potential guide dog is concerned, and we bear in mind also the sound parentage of the puppy which, when mature, will be considered for training. Sympathetic and thorough habituation additionally helps to give rise to equable temperament.

Just as philosophers, physicians and psychologists from the beginnings of civilisation have endeavoured to chart human temperament, with the evolvement of the domesticated dog canine character also has been much studied by breeders and behaviourists.

Hippocrates (460-370 B.C.) compared human temperament with physiological type. The body he considered as comprising the four elements of air, water, fire and earth, each corresponding to blood, phlegm and yellow bile and 'black bile'. Progressing on this theme, Galen (131-201 A.D.) felt that where one element predominated, this would govern temperamental type in man. Thus, he postulated, the sanguine or optimistic person would have an abundance of blood, the phlegmatic, slow and inactive person would have an excess of phlegm, a choleric or peppery individual would have much yellow bile, and the melancholic man would have a lot of 'black bile'.

More modern interpretations of character are less given to the mysticism of old and thus paint a reasonably clear and accurate picture of human temperament. The 20th Century American psychologist Thurstone mentions seven variables in character, viz., active, energetic, impetuous, degree of dominance in relations with others, stability, sociability, and inclination towards reflective theoretical pursuits.

* * * *

It is almost impossible and probably unwise to draw parallels between human and canine character, nevertheless, when we compare the chart of temperament (see figure 4-1) which has, over the years, been evolved to evaluate the disposition of the dog, it does bear a slight similarity, in one or two respects, with that of man. Just as we all have encountered the nervous, highly strung dog, so we have all met up with the highly strung, nervous man. And, as with the friendly, out-going person, so we have the friendly, out-going dog. Like man, some dogs are aggressive, and some are placid. Some can concentrate on a job of work for long periods at a time, others are easily distracted. No doubt other comparisons will spring to mind. So perhaps canine as well as other animal temperaments aren't as radically different from the character of man as we might at first imagine. But placing man infinitely beyond the minute animal mind are his superior intellect, powers of reasoning, and deep and extensive emotions. Only man can comprehend mortality and eternity. Only man can refine his mind to fulfil himself with cultural and artistic pursuits, to appreciate music, to read literature, to understand numeracy. Only man can look forward and plan for the future, and only man can look back at what has been and what might have been. The dog is a simple creature of the moment, but none the worse for that. And because of its unique - as far as the animal world is concerned - characteristic traits, the dog happily lends itself to be, among other things, a companion, guard and guide to its human associate.

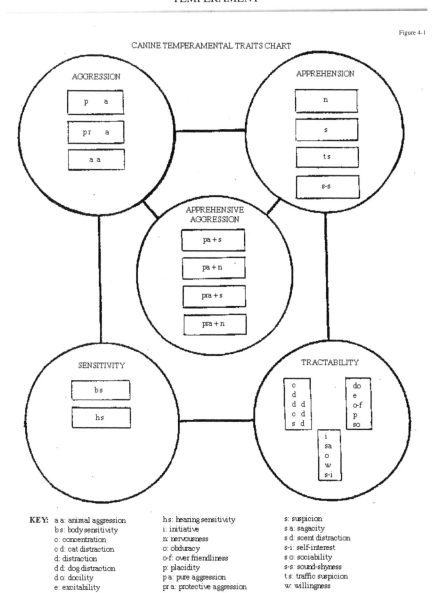

Figure 4-1

CANINE TEMPERAMENTAL TRAITS CHART

KEY:

a a: animal aggression	h s: hearing sensitivity	s: suspicion
b s: body sensitivity	i: initiative	s a: sagacity
c: concentration	n: nervousness	s d: scent distraction
c d: cat distraction	o: obduracy	s-i: self-interest
d: distraction	o-f: over friendliness	s o: sociability
d d: dog distraction	p: placidity	s-s: sound-shyness
d o: docility	p a: pure aggression	t s: traffic suspicion
e: excitability	pr a: protective aggression	w: willingness

47

CHARACTER

The character of the dog is classified under four main headings: Aggression, Apprehension, Sensitivity and Tractability. To be acceptable for training as a guide dog it is necessary, indeed vital, that in all sub-divisions of temperament the animal should be equable. It will be noted that temperamental traits do not stand alone; there is much overlap to finally form canine character.

As one of the main categories of character, Aggression is itself sub-divided into general (or pure) aggression, protective aggression and animal aggression (positive and negative). Although not considered a major category in itself, an important sub-division of canine disaffection is Apprehensive Aggression, which will emanate from one of the four components of pure aggression with suspicion, pure aggression with nervousness, protective aggression with suspicion, or protective aggression with nervousness.

Apprehension is sub-divided into suspicion, nervousness and sound-shyness, whilst Sensitivity appears as body sensitivity and hearing sensitivity. Tractability is identified with excitability, concentration, general distraction, dog distraction (positive and negative), cat distraction, scent distraction, willingness, self-interest, sociability, placidity, obduracy, docility, initiative (or sagacity) and over-friendliness.

AGGRESSION

General Aggression

Wild dogs living in a pack are inherently aggressive in order to regulate their position on the hierarchical scale within the group. The occasional (but not infrequent) skirmish results in a particular position being consolidated, vacated, or gained. Such skirmishes often break out among the lower positions in the pack. The pack-leader might be challenged less so. This post is occupied through superior power and sagacity, on which basis the human 'pack-leader' is countenanced by the dog which he handles. A dog which shows aggressive tendencies (usually, but not always, male, since it is they who more often than not fight for power within the pack, as well as playing a crucial part in the group's defences and attacks when the need arises) might decide to vent its feelings towards its owner and attack him, perhaps only through exhibition (growling and snarling) but sometimes bodily. This may be brought about, perhaps, by some show of attempted authority on the part of the handler; for example trying to make it carry out a command, such as "Sit", and the animal rebels against this. The owner, in such an instance, will need to forcefully assert his authority, and check the dog in no uncertain terms, by using brute strength if the confrontation calls for it. Should he not, and the dog is allowed to do as it will, then inevitably the animal will further assert itself on the grounds that it, and not the handler, is now the pack-leader.

Many years of domestication have thankfully quelled some of the wilder instincts in the dog, and so the out-and-out aggressive animal is seldom met up with. Nevertheless, one does come across such a dog, not showing aggression towards the owner, perhaps, but to other people, or groups of people; for example total strangers, or children. Any dog which exhibits aggression must be rejected. It would be a danger, if not to the owner then the public at large, if this canine liability were to be accepted for training as a guide dog.

Apprehensive Aggression

Frightened dogs will attack if there appears to be no other alternative avenue left open to them. Rather like the proverbial cornered rat, the terrified dog will bite an approaching stranger if it is unable to avoid the oncomer. It does so, not out of bravado or an attempt to assert authority, but because it is afraid; of what, it knows not. The attack of an apprehensive dog is not a sustained attack, as might be inflicted upon a person by an animal which is generally aggressive, but it is rather like the strike of a snake. The dog gives one bite, or parody of a bite, and then withdraws in the hope that the 'attacker' will do likewise. Where apprehensive aggression is evident in a dog, it will not be used as a guide. We have here a mix of undesirable temperamental traits and it is a combination which is not amenable to habituation or correction.

Protective Aggression

A dormant trait of the domesticated canine, and which still evidences itself in some, but by no means all dogs, is that of protective aggression. This stems from feral days when each member of a dog pack would be prepared, in company with its fellows, to protect the safety of the group against invasion and attack from outside marauders.

As well as protecting the pack, territory would also be sacrosanct. Thus it is that we all occasionally come across the dog which exhibits protective aggression whilst 'guarding' its master, and displays similar animosity towards strangers which the animal feels to be invading the 'pack's' territory, be it garden or house. Even small puppies can show protective aggression towards their food. Such behaviour should be instantly discouraged, and food bowls removed periodically whilst the dog is feeding, so that the puppy becomes aware that it must not show its teeth and snarl at those times when it mistakenly thinks its dinner is at risk.

In guide dog training protective tendencies are much frowned upon. The guide dog owner, now that he is very much part of the community, must always be approachable, without interference from an aggressive dog, by friends and strangers alike. If such an aggressive canine tendency shows signs of taking root at any time, the blind person must be most severe and correct the dog forthrightly the instant any animosity is displayed. If allowed to develop beyond control or correction, the dog would need to be withdrawn from guide work. It would reflect a poor light indeed on the guide dog agency concerned, should one of their products become aggressive to the point of attacking a member of the public, which could well be the ultimate outcome if protective aggression is allowed to grow unchecked.

Stern verbal and physical admonition by the handler should overcome a canine tendency to protective aggression. But where such therapy has no effect, the dog should be rejected.

Animal Aggression

Some dogs are aggressive towards other animals. They might attack chickens or sheep, for instance, and stern measures must be adopted to quell this extreme habit. Violent correction at the precise moment of misdemeanour is vital. A dog which is temperamentally sound in all other directions might still be considered for training where they have this one fault of animal aggression, but only on the understanding that punitive measures totally subvert the vice. The dog which is aggressive towards other dogs must similarly be disciplined, and only where desired results are forthcoming will guide dog training be envisaged.

A dog might only appear to be aggressive in that it is prepared to chase an animal which will flee from it, but if that animal turns and stands its ground the canine will desist from aggression. The dog showing positive animal aggression is however a fighter out-and-out. Both negative and positive aggressive tendencies must be suppressed for guide dog training to be successful.

APPREHENSION

The apprehensive canine displays uneasiness, and perhaps fear, which, to a greater or lesser extent fills the dog with dread. This affects the animal's receptivity to training, or indeed, acceptance for guide dog work in the first place.

Nervousness

A nervous dog is of little use as a guide. However, with habituation to the modern environment a number of nervous dogs do become steadier and less prone to attacks of shyness when confronted with situations of stress. The archetypal signs of nervousness in a dog are attacks of shivering and shrinking away from the source of concern; at its worst, the animal takes acute fright and runs away wildly not knowing whither it is going. Such a dog would be rejected as unsuitable for training since even if attempts were made to accustom it to the cause of its attacks of nervousness, the time spent in so doing (and success not necessarily being the outcome) would be unwarranted.

Suspicion

The malformed Richard III, in Shakespeare's play, describes himself thusly: "Deformed, unfinished, sent before my time into this breathing world, scarce half made up, and that so lamely and unfashionable that dogs bark at me as I halt by them".

The errant dogs which barked at the unfortunate Richard as he limped past them exhibited indisputable signs of that temperamental trait we know as suspicion. Most dogs react uncertainly towards situations and sights that are out-of-the-ordinary. But because a dog is used to the presence of 'ordinary' people, because it has been habituated to humans since it was a puppy, it does not react unfavourably to them. However, a suspicious animal will continue to look askance at all persons other than those well known to it throughout its life-time. Such a creature may make a useful watch-dog, but, unless the suspicion is of a mild nature, it will be of little use as a guide and thus would warrant rejection. A guide dog needs to be approachable and at least reasonably friendly, or indifferent, to all the many people it comes into contact with during its everyday work. A suspicious dog might deter people from approaching, or being approached by, the guide dog owner, and guiding propensity will be adversely affected if it is suspicious of animate or inanimate objects whilst working in harness.

Those dogs which were suspicious of King Richard may not, however, have been beyond redemption. If the king had taken the trouble to stop awhile, and allowed individual dogs to approach him, and if he had spoken kindly to the animal as the creature investigated him, and if in this way he had attempted to make friends with the canine without pressing his favours upon it, before long the dog would have realised that there was nothing to be afraid of in this 'extraordinary' person and, possibly, its suspicion would have been allayed. This is so of many dogs; at first, they may be suspicious of people or objects which appear strange to them, but once they have investigated the person or artefact and are satisfied that all is well, then they are no longer dubious as far as this particular scene is concerned. Their suspicion may not disappear overnight, but with repeated confrontations of the objects of their anxiety, the trait will gradually fade. If it does not, the animal must be rejected.

A peculiar form of fear affecting dogs which perhaps in the past have suffered trauma when confronted by motor vehicles is the phenomenon known as *traffic suspicion*. Maybe venomous car exhausts blasting into a canine face, or thundering heavy lorries in extreme close proximity, have brought about this fear of traffic. With sympathetic habituation to busy traffic conditions in the hands of a considerate trainer, traffic suspicion may be overcome. If not, rejection looks ominous.

Sound-Shyness

Dogs which fall prostrate to the ground with fear at the sound of exploding cap-guns, thunder, cars back-firing and similar noises must be rejected.

Sound-shyness should not, indeed could not, be confused with high hearing sensitivity. A dog with high hearing sensitivity does not become fearful of the noise it hears, whereas the sound-shy dog is overcome with frenzy at a loud explosion. A sound-shy dog will seldom fully conquer this fear, and should be rejected. Otherwise, if trained and allocated to a blind person, on the occasion it hears a loud report guide dog performance would be both abysmal and unsafe, since a sound-shy animal takes some little while in recovering from its fright, during which time it would be totally unable to work as it should.

SENSITIVITY

Hearing Sensitivity

With few exceptions, the dog is peculiarly receptive to the human voice, a facility which is fostered by the trainer and which develops into an irreplaceable means of human communication directed towards the canine. Although primarily a one-way projection since only the man directs his utterances to the dog without sophisticated reciprocation, nevertheless there is some semblance of vocal communication by the animal when one considers, for example, the whining of the canine which wants a drink, or a door opened, or when a warning bark is sounded. Other vocal intonations used by dogs in an effort to impart meaning, usually towards individual owners who, through familiarity, would understand these rudimentary signals, could be instanced many times over.

We are concerned here, however, with canine receptivity of the human voice. To coin a phrase, "It's not what you say, it's the way that you say it". The dog does not understand words as such, it is the intonation of the voice which conveys the message. Of course, over a period of time, these intonations come to mean something to the dog, in which case, it might be claimed, it begins to understand simple speech, or rather, individual words. In fact, the first word the dog grows to recognise is its own name.

With time and training the dog begins to associate the intonation of words with specific objectives. "Walk", "Dinner", "Chemist", "Church", "Pub", and so on, so that as the partnership evolves a blind person can build up quite a repertoire of words (usually associated with particular destinations) which his guide dog appears to understand. It may only recognise these utterances (or the intonation of them) when they are spoken by its handler. Because of the differences in the individual voices, words spoken by another person may not be comprehended by the dog.

However, over a comparatively short space of time, the animal will begin to appreciate the verbal commands of a person other than the original handler. This helps account for the relatively trouble-free take-over of a guide dog (with some exceptions) by the student when the training of the two together is first effected. Because of the increasingly close affinity of guide dog owner and guide dog, scope for advancement of word appreciation by the canine is unlimited as time goes on, and the two develop a deepening relationship.

As far as hearing sensitivity is concerned, those dogs with a high receptivity might be considered to be more discerning with regard to the comprehension of words. This does not necessarily follow. The degree of hearing sensitivity does, however, determine the manner in which the handler corrects each individual dog.

A dog of high hearing sensitivity, for instance, will be responsive to the slightest admonition imparted by voice, and similarly so to any subsequent countermanding verbal praise, whilst an animal of low hearing sensitivity may call for severe vocal chastisement and a concentrated delivery of warm words before some response is indicated. However, although only a brief word of praise might suffice for the highly hearing dog, in order to gain and keep its confidence, the handler may be advised to maintain whispered encouragement almost constantly. Conversely, since the dog with low hearing sensitivity may well be unconcerned with words of praise, and if the handler fails to elicit a show of response no matter the feeling and variation in his verbal terms of endearment, it might be as well to dispense with these altogether - in respect of this particular animal – rather than have such congenial utterances fall on deaf ears, so to speak.

In the case of low canine hearing sensitivity, negative reinforcement by way of relentless scolding words should be applied forcibly when the situation warrants it, together with physical correction if need be. However, a dog with such a low hearing sensitivity that it pays no heed to words of praise or correction may need to be rejected, unless, that is, it can still be conditioned to performing the various tasks of a guide dog without apparent encouragement or discouragement.

Where a dog's hearing sensitivity is so high that it borders on sound-shyness; that is, a car back-firing, a jet plane roaring overhead, a cap gun report, a pneumatic drill in operation, or similar noises, startle the animal to the extent that it becomes acutely disturbed and takes some while to recover, then this dog will have to be rejected. If it is only slightly upset, however, and recovers composure almost immediately, and is satisfactory in all other respects, then this dog could be a suitable subject for training.

Body Sensitivity

Two extremes of body sensitivity may present themselves when analysing the temperament of the dog. A dog with a low body sensitivity is a 'hard' animal which pays little respect to physical correction. A dog such as this is unsuitable for training as a guide since, although the trainer may be able to effect response from the animal by inflicting a severe correction to stop canine recalcitrance, it is unfair, even if possible, to ask a blind person to do the same should such an animal be allocated to him. Also, the general populace would not look so kindly upon a person, whether blind or sighted, imposing what might appear to them excessive punishment (notwithstanding the fact that the dog, because of its low body sensitivity, is well able to withstand such 'punishment') upon a working dog.

At the other end of the scale is the 'soft' dog, the one with high body sensitivity. An animal such as this will flinch unreservedly at the slightest hint of physical admonishment. Often (but not always) a 'soft' dog also has high hearing sensitivity, and consequently verbal correction will suffice. Unfortunately, however, its high body sensitivity means that it will not be too prepared to endure the physical knocks and contact which a guide dog must inevitably suffer in its day to day routine.

Not only will the 'soft' dog, when at work, shy away from its handler fearful of a trodden paw or some other bodily collision, but it is also wary of other pedestrians to the extent, especially in crowds of people, it will try to leave a wide berth between them and it, and by doing so might endanger the blind person. In other words, the animal is so concerned about protecting its own physique that it is forgetful of the handler who, ostensibly, it has been trained to protect. These factors thus render a dog with high body sensitivity unsuitable for training.

Ideally, the potential guide dog will have a body sensitivity that is neither too high nor too low. Preferably, the dog will incline, but not overmuch, to a higher body sensitivity rather than a lower.

It is true that a dog with high body sensitivity might have this trait lowered, over a period of time, by a gradually increasing application of physical correction which the animal is just able to withstand, until such occasion as it begins to resist each successive but slightly increasing degree of correction. It is similarly true that a 'hard' dog can have its body sensitivity heightened by over-correction, but this must be administered judiciously and to a finite degree.

Dogs which have had their body sensitivities heightened or lowered by such training techniques will need to be allocated with care to particular blind persons, who themselves will need to be prudent handlers since, in the wrong hands, these original temperamental traits of the animals might revert to their previous and undesirable levels.

TRACTABILITY

A tractable (or biddable) dog is one which is easily handled and manageable. It is a patient non-wilful animal which is receptive to training and anxious to please the handler and do his bidding. The tractable dog is encouraged during training to exercise its sagacity, or initiative, to the extent that it must, within the limitations of the canine mind, accept a modicum of decision-making. This is exemplified particularly when finding destinations, and dealing with obstacles and traffic, and crowds of people.

A glance at the Canine Temperamental Traits Chart reveals that tractability covers many aspects of the dogs' character, some desirable others undesirable, but all of them important in guide dog training.

Distraction

Although the main source of distraction to a dog is, more often than not, the sight, sound or smell of its fellow, there are many other founts of interest to capture canine attention. The first two in the list of distractions, besides another dog, are invariably of a feline or olfactory nature.

To offset interest in cats, it is useful if the future guide dog is reared in a home where a feline is present. Even so, canine curiosity in other cats may still not be contained when it is out walking and a strange feline springs into view. Stern correction may be called for. Similarly with scent distraction; the dog must be prevented from stopping and sniffing during a walk. Undue cat and scent distraction which doesn't respond to a modicum of correction will spell rejection for the dog which is in the process of being tested as to suitability for training. Where the dog responds to censure, however, and now ignores the former source of inattention, all other things being equal, it will be well worth accepting.

Many are the other distractions in which a dog might pay illicit interest. Farm animals, pigeons, people, children at play, balls and stones being thrown about, leaves blowing in the breeze, water gushing from a fountain, and scores of other such sights and sounds may attract the attention of a dog undergoing testing or training. Only when it is responsive to the wishes of the handler should training continue. A little canine disinterest in its duties from time to time, is well within the capacity of the average blind person to deal with, but uncontrollable distraction warrants rejection.

Positive Dog Distraction.

Dogs naturally show interest in other dogs. Where a dog is being trained to do a job of work, such as guiding a blind person, it must always keeps its attention on the job in hand, and therefore interest in other dogs (whilst it is working in harness) must be discouraged. Most dogs show a positive interest in other canines; that is to say, when they see another dog they pull towards it, in order to ascertain gender, and whether friend or foe. This distraction must be discouraged forthrightly by the handler; he will jerk the lead and admonish the animal verbally. Once the dog responds by ignoring the other animal, the handler praises it for so doing. Ideally, the guide dog walks at a steady pace past all other dogs, no matter whether they are loose or on a lead, without faltering or looking at, or moving towards, another dog. If such indications of interest are evident, then the handler admonishes his charge accordingly. Correction must be counterbalanced bearing in mind the dog's sensitivity, since over-correction can bring about the negative form of dog distraction.

Negative Dog Distraction

The dog which tries to give a wide berth to another dog it is passing is a little apprehensive about the outcome of a confrontation with the other animal, and therefore skirts it. Sometimes the amount of leeway which it wishes to leave between it and the other animal is excessive, to the extent it may even abandon the pavement and go into the road to afford itself security. Such a degree of negative dog distraction is to be looked upon with concern, since obviously it possibly places the handler in a position of some danger. Where a dog walks into the roadway in order to avoid another of its own kind, the handler becomes vulnerable to passing vehicles. Also, the animal may be so besotted by its own need to keep a respectable distance from other dogs, that the quality of its right shoulder work (that is, adequate clearance for the owner alongside) is affected to a degree where the safety of the handler becomes secondary.

To help overcome negative dog distraction, which, except in extreme cases is by no means an insurmountable task, words of reassurance and conciliation should help placate the dog and give it confidence when another animal is approached, and such encounters, after a while, will become of little concern to the canine. Where warm words fail to evoke a fading of negative dog distraction, however, rejection may unfortunately be the only answer.

Concentration

In order to achieve a high standard of capability and safety, a guide dog must concentrate upon the work in hand to the exclusion of outside influences. A dog with poor concentration will remain interested in the many sights and sounds that surround it during its daily tasks. Even when the animal is roundly corrected by the handler, the level of concentration stays weak and ensuing performance is poor. Lack of concentration is akin to general distraction, where the animal is unable to devote itself to the wishes of the handler, and persists in having its attention diverted by sounds, sights and smells which it should totally ignore whilst working.

A dog with a good level of concentration will adopt a posture which implies devotion to duty as it guides its handler. It will hold its head reasonably high, with ears back or dropped, looking hardly to left or right as it walks comfortably along, at a pace suited to the handler, and responding in the way it has been conditioned to those stimuli offered it which are relevant to guide dog work.

Initiative

A guide dog, on behalf of its master, must find pedestrian crossings, bus stops, shops, friends' and relatives' houses, offices, factories, exits and entrances, flights of steps, telephone kiosks, post boxes, and scores of other points and ports of call where the blind person will wish to be taken. Therefore, dogs for training must show a fair amount of sagacity. After one or two visits, a guide dog, at mention of the word, for instance, "Chemist", when uttered by its owner during a walk in the vicinity of this shop, will immediately make for the destination requested.

With patience and perseverance, and with a dog of some initiative, a blind person can help develop the animal's perspicacity to quite an astonishing degree. Even after long lapses of time, a dog will find a particular port of call, perhaps months after the last visit, when requested to do so. On the other hand, it may find a destination when not asked to do so! This, however, is of little consequence, since all the blind person needs to do is whisper, "Come on silly dog, we don't want to go there today", and encourage the dog to continue.

Identifying destinations is, of course, only one aspect of canine initiative. Some sagacity is called for in most facets of training, coupled with the conditioning implemented by the trainer. Initiative, alone, however, does not necessarily make for good guiding quality. The dog must be well-trained and of sound temperament besides.

Sociability

No matter how well-trained to work as a guide dog in harness, it is not much use for a blind person if that dog is badly-behaved when meeting people or visiting different places socially. No jumping up, no going out of its way to seek the attention of both friends and strangers, no begging for tit-bits, no restlessness when told to stay under a table whilst its owner and his companions enjoy a cup of tea in a cafe, no noisy outbursts at odd intervals whilst the blind person is conversing with others, and no straining at the lead in impatience; in short, perfect social behaviour at all times.

Placidity

In the midst of the hurly-burly of everyday life, the panic of pedestrians rushing hither and thither, the maelstrom of churning traffic in fume-ridden city streets, the horror of a nearby car smash, the disturbance of dogs fighting in the street, the attraction of children playing on the pavements, the guide dog is calm and unperturbed. No matter the crisis or the confusion, in the company of its master the well-trained, temperamentally sound guide dog remains placid and unconcerned, and quietly and efficiently gets on with its work.

Docility

As with placidity, docility in a potential guide dog is much to be desired. A docile dog is receptive to training and is equable and unruffled under conditions of stress. Countermanding docility is *over-friendliness*. Far better for a guide dog to be aloof to the approaches of strangers (and indeed friends, whilst working) than to be over-friendly. The fawning dog often proves to be an embarrassment to the guide dog owner; furthermore, the standard of work is affected because of the dogs over-friendly overtures. The same applies to the excitable dog which, if its *excitability* cannot be moderated during training, will warrant rejection.

Obduracy

An excess of initiative might lead to obduracy. For instance, the dog might insist on going to a destination it has been to in the past, and no amount of insistence by a blind handler will deflect the dog from its course. Similarly, where the dog has always turned right at a road junction in the past, and now the handler wants to turn left, the dog might be obdurate in the extreme and resist the handler's efforts to make it go to the left. Obduracy, however, is not a serious fault and by persistence and patience on the part of the handler can usually be overcome.

Self-interest

There are those dogs which are so concerned with what they can get for themselves that they are oblivious to the wishes of the handler - if they can escape with it. Such animals need a firm hand. Often, they are otherwise temperamentally sound, and consequently perfectly capable of, once trained, performing well as a guide, given the effective control of the handler, and accepting the fact that there may be certain limitations to beware of. For instance, a dog with a lot of self-interest, if it is allowed to do so, will socially misbehave. It will jump up at people and look for tit-bits; it will scavenge around rooms, and parks and pavements if running loose, seeking food. Indeed, even in harness it is liable to do likewise, and divert attention to anything which takes its fancy; that is, if the handler doesn't prevent it, with sharp and timely reminders, from indulging in its wilful ways.

Furthermore, when running free, it may be reluctant to return to hand when called. Where a dog is persistently disobedient in this respect, it should not be allowed any liberty. It should always be contained on a long lead when exercising in field or park. In the wrong hands, a dog full of self-interest can be a bit of a liability to a blind person. Such a dog must therefore be carefully matched to a firm and strong-willed individual who can readily exert appropriate authority over this selfish animal.

<u>Willingness</u>

A dog which is reluctant to perform the tasks for which it is being trained could be quite a handful and a handicap for the eventual user. A guide dog should be willing, at all times, to go out to work in harness with its owner for whatever the duration of the walk, and where-ever the destinations. It should go willingly at the speed it has been trained to walk to accommodate the user, and be responsive to his wishes should an increase or decrease in pace be called for.

An initially unwilling dog can be compelled to walk briskly to suit the trainer, and later the animal may find that it is now enjoying the work after all, and consequently willingness increases of its own volition. A dog which is too willing may travel at an excessive pace and so its enthusiasm will need curbing. An unwilling dog will be reluctant to leave on an outward trip, but may pull on the return journey. Dogs also head for home at an uncontrollable speed however, in some instances, in the expectation of food almost as soon as they step indoors. In such cases, the guide dog owner should allow at least an hour to elapse before feeding his charge, in order to lessen the liability of being towed home by a powerful, greedy tug on four legs.

With the unwilling dog, to make it lead ahead in the correct guide dog position in relation to the handler, one must speak encouragingly to the animal with eager, excited words. Run, skip and jump alongside, and delight the dog: jangle the lead, and it will respond by quickening its pace. For the really recalcitrant mover, some negative reinforcement might be indicated: scolding words, "Get on with it, you bad boy. Hurry up", and a measure of physical compulsion with upward and forward jerks of the handle, all of which must be judiciously applied only as a last resort, since, to increase willingness, it is better to employ positive reinforcement to gain desired results. Introducing a pleasant port of call to the walk, such as playtime in the park, for instance, can also help. The best remedy by far, however, is the indefinable personality of the handler, through which rapport with the dog is achieved, and the animal works willingly and responsively purely for the pleasure of being with, to canine eyes, this splendid person. Where a dog's willingness is so high that it travels at too fast a pace, speed control, the application of which is described elsewhere, should be utilised. For the dog which pulls to the extreme, there are on the market proprietary makes of canine halters that might help to curb excessive speed.

5

TESTING AND ASSESSMENT

Dogs used for training as guides must be physically fit, at least 18 inches high at the shoulder, and temperamentally sound. At the start of training they should be aged between 12 and 30 months. Older dogs could be used (some animals with previous experience as a guide dog, aged perhaps three to five years, are occasionally assigned to the older or more incapacitated applicant) but this reduces the length of time they will be of service to a blind person.

The majority of guide dogs are Labrador retrievers, some yellow, some black, and a very small minority chocolate. Of the remainder, German shepherd dogs (Alsatians) and golden retrievers predominate, with individual animals such as curly coated retrievers, flat coated retrievers, Airedale terriers, collies, cross breeds and occasional others being turned out as guide dogs.

The Labrador is very much the utility dog of guide dog training. It is, usually, a placid, patronising beast, lacking a little, perhaps, in initiative, but with few temperamental discrepancies. It is of good proportion physically, has a shortish coat, and is a resilient dog which suffers few ailments. The major drawback of most Labradors is that they are greedy, and might be inclined to scavenging when the opportunity presents itself; and they are often over-friendly, a fault which can adversely affect their work in harness if they pay attention to a drooling passer-by.

The German shepherd dog not infrequently presents itself as slightly suspicious of people, to the extent of apparent aggression. This aloofness towards strangers is, however, an asset in a guide dog. It also seems prone to traffic suspicion and, strangely perhaps, often appears to be of higher sensitivity than the Labrador. Additionally, the shepherd dog is quite perceptive, and thus reads the moods (albeit a good trainer should be of a constant and amenable disposition) of the handler fairly readily. Being more of a one man dog, it is not inclined to wander whilst running free, as might a Labrador. The German shepherd dog is not as easily matched with a blind person when compared to the Labrador but, if temperamentally sound and in the right hands, it can make a first-class guide dog.

The golden retriever combines many of the qualities of both Labrador and German shepherd, but can be rather an obdurate animal not given easily to change; for instance, it might take unkindly to an alteration in a familiar route. Its long coat means more vacuuming for the owner, but in most circumstances the golden retriever trains well and, as a guide dog, leaves little to be desired. When crossed with the Labrador, here again we have the makings of a good guide dog.

Many collies are unfortunately short in stature, but the larger ones which are sound enough for training prove to be willing, adaptable and sagacious guide dogs. They are responsive to the owner, show a lot of initiative, and have an excellent memory for routes and ports of call.

Over 55 per cent of guide dogs are bitches. These are spayed, mostly after the first or second seasons are spent. Bitches are commonly used because, in the main, they are biddable, more affectionate, less likely to stray, less likely to be interested in other dogs, less likely to be aggressive, less likely to have canine odours, less likely to be 'hard', slightly less likely to be interested in smelling the areas where other animals have been, more likely to be equable and, additionally, they don't stop at intermittent intervals to lift a hind leg and decorate posts and trees in the inimitable manner the uncastrated male would do. However, those male dogs used for training are castrated at that crucial stage of development before the onset of permanent masculine canine characteristics as described, and therefore prove the equal of bitches with regard to guide dog work.

We have discussed the procedures of socialisation and habituation in the chapter on puppy-walking, and elsewhere. Dogs which arrive from the puppy-walker for testing as to their suitability for training as guides therefore stand an excellent chance of acceptability as, in their formative months, the animals will have been adequately socialised and habituated. Since they will also have originated from breeding stock which has proved to be temperamentally suitable in the past, this too helps to account for the high success rate of puppy-walked dogs insofar as acceptability and ultimate training success is concerned. Temperament we have also discussed in another chapter, so we are well aware of the desirable traits which should present themselves when an animal is tested for appositeness to begin guide dog training.

Physique, socialisation, habituation and temperament are therefore crucial factors to be aware of, and to determine that they are positively present when testing a potential guide dog. Because puppy-walked dogs have been closely monitored during development by the puppy-walking supervisor, and thus faulty animals will have been weeded out before arriving for assessment at the training centre, the trainer's task is made that much easier by this influx of suitable raw guide dog material.

Not all guide dogs, however, originate from puppy-walking sources. A number of organisations rely, to varying extents, on adult dogs which might be presented or sold to them by owners who now find themselves in a position where they can no longer provide a home for their pets. Moving house, another addition to the family, a pup grown to be bigger than at first thought, unable to keep pace with the financial implications of looking after a large dog, these and other reasons will account for an owner offering his pet to a training agency for consideration as a guide.

Some of these animals make first-rate candidates for training. Regrettably, they are in a minority. Only about 25 per cent of dogs offered to training organisations from this avenue prove to be acceptable. As well as the reasons enumerated for an owner offering his pet dog for training as a guide, unfortunately some less-scrupulous, or (to be kinder) less-knowledgeable persons offer animals which bear undesirable traits. A dog which might have bitten the postman, for instance, or an animal which is sound-shy. A dog which is excitable and unmanageable. A dog which chases sheep, or is besotted with cats. All or one of these traits would obviously render a dog unsuitable for acceptance. So the training agency relies to a great extent on the honesty and integrity of a fond owner offering his pet for training as a guide. But it will rely even further on the assessment procedures which ensue in the hands of a skilled trainer, who will then make a decision as to rejecting or accepting the dog for training.

Foremost in the trainer's mind whilst testing a canine candidate will be those four vital subject areas of physique, socialisation, habituation and temperament, with the greater emphasis laid upon the latter. After all, a thin, undernourished dog can have its physique and health improved by adequate diet and care. And dogs which are not too well socialised or habituated can, during training, have any blanks in these two respects filled in, so long as they do not leave much to be overcome in such vital fields. Temperament, however, is of rather a different order. An aggressive dog, once mature, cannot be made - with absolute safety guaranteed - friendly. A sound-shy dog cannot be made complacent in the face of loud noise. And a highly-strung adult dog cannot be made placid.

A dog for testing need not have been conditioned in any way to suit the requirements of guiding. This is going to be done by the trainer. All he needs is the raw material to work on. Yet even where temperament is lacking, due allowance must be made for improvement as time and training progresses. A dog with a high body sensitivity, for instance, with prudent handling can have this sensitivity moderated. Similarly a dog at the other extreme, with low body sensitivity. A suspicious dog can have its dubious nature improved; a nervous dog might become bolder; a dog showing signs of protection can have this tendency eradicated. A dog with negative or positive dog distraction can be helped to overcome these faults, and a dog which is traffic suspicious can be encouraged to ignore this source of fear.

Thus, during testing the trainer will be observant regarding those temperamental areas which would render a dog totally unsuitable for guide work (e.g., aggression, uncontrollable excitability, sound-shyness) and those areas where, so long as the fault is of a minor nature and only moderately developed, (e.g., slight suspicion, some nervousness, dog distraction, traffic suspicion) acceptance is indicated, but only where the animal does not have too many of these faults cumulatively, and where he feels, with a measure of time and patience, the faults will disappear.

With reference to the list of canine temperamental traits, the trainer will be closely observing the demeanour of an 'approval' dog (approval since, if unsuitable, the animal will be returned to the original owner, whilst rejected puppy-walked dogs are sent back to the walker. If owner or walker do not want their original charges back, the dogs are sold as pets) and, during the testing and assessment period of three weeks, have the animal face a multitude of situations in order to decide upon suitability.

He will walk the dog along quiet streets and teeming thoroughfares. Down country lanes and alongside roads dense with traffic. He will visit shops, schools and factories; bus stations and railway stations; travel on public transport; walk up and down steps, over bridges and through tunnels. The dog will meet numerous other animals and people. It will hear the noise of pneumatic drills and starting pistols. It will ride on lifts and alongside escalators. It will go into cafes, offices and houses. In short, during testing it will meet up with every conceivable environmental feature that the modern world presents, and in the face of these features, ideally, it will remain complacent and unmoved, upon which the trainer will have little hesitation in accepting this animal for training as a guide dog.

As an added bonus, the guide dog-to-be will be adequately socialised, of moderate to slightly high body sensitivity, of a well-proportioned physique, be biddable and responsive to the dictates of the handler, be totally habituated to our everyday world, be friendly but not over-demonstrative towards strangers, be ready to ignore outside distractions, preferring to keep its attention upon the needs of its master, be of good concentration whilst out walking, ignoring other dogs and animals, and remaining placid under conditions of stress.

Such are the rigorous requirements of guide dog material. Only a small minority of dogs present themselves in this near-perfect way. Thus the trainer will accept also animals of a lesser light, knowing that adequate and skilful training, socialisation, habituation and conditioning will moderate some, if not all, of the faults.

The trainer must beware, however, of accepting a dog which falls below minimum standards of suitability. He might be prepared, for instance, to accept a faulty dog because it happens to be an endearing one. He must not let his heart rule his head. Emotion must not play a part in testing. Rigid adherence to at least reasonably high standards of acceptability must be maintained. Dogs with temperamental and other faults should only be accepted where the defects are minor, not cumulative, and have every chance of being overcome with the influence of time and training. To accept less is unfair on the animal, reflects badly upon the agency and upon the trainer concerned and, worst of all, is dishonest to the blind person who will eventually be asked to handle and work with this isolated inferior dog.

6

OBEDIENCE

To be effective as a guide dog, the animal should first be well versed in obedience training. Not to the extent that it is a budding obedience champion, since some of the niceties of such training are not strictly required of a guide dog anyway (such as heel work and retrieving), but certainly to a degree where it is promptly responsive to the words of command "Sit", "Down", "Stay" and "Come", all of which are practised out of harness, the introduction of this fixture being discussed later. In harness, the wearing of which is specifically geared to guide dog duties only, perhaps two of these commands might now and then be used, namely "Sit", and possibly "Stay".

When in harness, the dog is not encouraged to lie down, and, similarly, the recall will not be required when the fixture is worn, since a dog in harness is not allowed to run loose anyway. For all free exercise and general obedience training, the harness is removed. This helps to preserve the work ethic associated with the harness by the dog when it is affixed to the animal prior to embarking upon a walk in its capacity as a guide.

As far as sitting is concerned, again, in harness, it is not imperative that the dog should adopt such a posture, no matter whether at a down-kerb, or at the master's side whilst he is standing chatting to a friend, or being served in a shop. It is quite permissible, indeed perhaps advisable, for the dog to stand. Nevertheless, the guide dog must be trained to sit in quick response to the verbal command. By being responsive to general obedience commands, it helps instil discipline and respect for the owner's authority which rubs off in improved guide dog performance.

Obedience training will precede (it can be practised with the growing puppy), and subsequently be undertaken concurrently with, guide dog work, during any convenient interval of time. Such exercises should be comparatively short but intensive, say 30 to 60 minutes, and should conclude with a brief, enjoyable romp involving both dog and man. Play also has its place in formulating the bond and special relationship between a particular person and his dog.

Upon the word of command "Sit" the dog instantly does so. At first, the animal obviously cannot comprehend the meaning of the word, and therefore must be compelled physically to obey. The right hand grasps the dog, which is on the left, under the chest - this is a restraining grip, to stop the animal moving forward in an effort to avoid the sitting posture - whilst the left hand presses the dog's hindquarters to the ground, tucking the rear legs under it as it does so, at the same time issuing a sharp word of command, "Sit".

With the dog beginning to appreciate the injunction's implication the right hand on the chest can be dispensed with, and a slight upward jerk on the lead, together with pressure on the animal's rear with the left hand should suffice to elicit the response, again accompanied by the word of command.

As soon as the order "Sit" is given, the dog must be made to do so. The command should be uttered only once, and the dog, if it doesn't do it of its own volition, must be instantly made to respond. It is no good saying "Sit; sit; sit; sit....", incessantly repeating the command to deaf ears in the vague hope of the dog acceding to your wishes; repetitive orders without compulsion to have them carried out will only serve to encourage the animal to ignore them. With effective physical negative reinforcement, associated with the one word of command, it should not be too long before the dog is responding appropriately.

A word of praise, but no physical caresses, suffices as positive reinforcement. If, however, the dog attempts to move or get up in response to praise, the animal is immediately returned to the sitting position manually and terms of endearment are dispensed with.

The dog must remain sitting until ordered otherwise. General obedience training is usually carried out on a greensward, and since the dog is not working in harness, rather than the command "Forward" the words "Get on" can be used to have the dog move off from the sitting position. Without pulling, the dog still maintains tension on the lead, and in so doing continues providing a measure of guidance to the person on its right. Indeed, the handler may call upon the initiative of the dog to find the "Bench" if in the park, or the "Gate" which leads out of it, or the "Door" of the house if obedience training has just concluded in the garden.

It is useful on numerous occasions to have the dog lying down upon hearing the appropriate word of command, such as on public transport, when told to lie in its basket, or when visiting friends and the animal must recline quietly without making any fuss or noise.

The dog, initially, is told to sit. From this position, the command "Down" is given, and a downward jerk on the lead is applied, together with pressure on the forequarters. Alternatively, since sometimes the dog digs its feet into the ground, and it is then difficult to gain the desired effect with pressure on the forequarters, the front legs can be grasped and pulled forward (or to one side) so that the animal has no choice but to lie down. In these early stages it is immaterial as to which posture the dog adopts whilst recumbent, whether on its back or side, or, ideally, sphinx-like. Before long, of its own accord, it will assume the latter Egyptian pose.

Therefore it matters little about the method of physical compulsion, or of the manner in which the dog lies down when it is prostrate, so long as the exercise is completed to accompany the one word of command "Down". Once effected, the dog is not praised since it will try to rise in response to this. If it does try to get up, it is forcibly pushed to the ground again.

The more sensitive animal might wonder what on earth is going on when such efforts are made to push it to the ground, which is why many dogs react by trying to spring up again. But once the meaning of the exercise is beginning to be understood, the response is ready. Again, one word of command only to be issued, and once the animal is responding to the down from the sitting position, it can be practised from a standing posture. Any signs of dalliance on the dog's part when commands are issued should be countered by negative reinforcement.

Due to insufficient or incorrect training, some dogs consistently misbehave. A dog has no comprehension, as we have, between right and wrong. There is no code of ethics which the dog understands in human terms, so it is left to the owner to decide what the animal may do and may not do. Faults in a dog are often the faults of the owner.

To rectify certain vices in a dog may entail the use of strict compulsion; so strict, in fact, that the owner, naturally being fond of the animal, may hesitate to apply the treatment. If this is the case, then the fault will quite obviously have to be lived with, in the certain knowledge that it will probably worsen as time goes on.

Most people have encountered the dog which does not come when it is called. We may have met with the owner in the park exercising his pet. The dog is careering gaily about, while the owner, calling in vain, issues dire threats as to the fate of the dog when eventually it does come to hand.

Ultimately, the dog returns or is captured, and the threats are duly carried out. The dog is being punished in the mistaken belief that it knows the reason for the punishment. The owner believes the dog will understand that the punishment is because it did not come when it was called. Nothing could be further from the truth. Having come to hand, the dog thinks that this is the cause for castigation. Consequently the situation is aggravated, and the dog becomes more and more reluctant to answer the entreaties of its master. Eventually, the dog is completely hand-shy, believing - rightly - that if it does return to the owner then it will be punished.

To have the dog willing to come to hand when called, it is absolutely essential to praise it each and every time it returns. No matter how long the lapse in time between calling and the eventual return, the dog must always be praised. Even if a misdeed is committed between the call and return, praise must still be given. In order to punish the dog for the misdeed which happened in the meanwhile, it must be taken to the scene of the crime and - only if the misdeed can be associated with the punishment - chastised there.

As an example, the dog is running free in a field, and it is decided to recall it. But while returning it chances upon a free-range chicken, kills it, and then returns to hand. The dog is praised upon its return, and then taken to the carcass of the hen. The dog is shown the fowl and chastised. The bird is picked up and the dog is beaten about the head and muzzle with it. In this way the animal is taught to differentiate between right and wrong. It is right to come to hand, for which it will be praised, but it is wrong to kill chickens, for which it will be punished.

A dog which will stay in a given spot without demur, in the corner of a room, or under a table, or in its bed, is a necessary requirement for a blind person. This exercise ties in with general obedience training. At first, the dog is taken outside to a place free from an undue amount of distraction, and there made to sit, or lie down. The command "Stay" is uttered, the word being made long and drawn out and spoken with authority. The lead remains affixed as the handler walks slowly away from the dog for a metre or two. If the dog attempts to move, it is quickly and roughly replaced in the self-same position as before. It can be expedient to repeat the verbal command "Stay", the very intonation of the word implying that the animal must not move from the allotted spot. Initially, the handler takes care not to jerk the lead, since the dog may interpret this as a signal to move. Later, when the dog is steady in the stay position, the lead will be deliberately jerked to encourage the animal to remain where it is no matter the inducement, to await and respond only to the verbal recall.

In the preliminary stages of the stay exercise, with the lead still in use, the handler, having issued the command, goes away to the full extent of the rein, and circles slowly round the animal. With the dog becoming steadier at the stay with each passing lesson, the handler gets up to all sorts of antics at which the animal remains steadfast, responding only to the one command "Come". But before that recall exercise, the handler returns to the dog and praises it for staying resourcefully in the way it has.

For the important recall lesson, in which the dog is trained to come to hand when called, initially the dog is in the stay position, but still on the lead. The handler walks away as far as the lead allows, turns round and waits awhile (so that the dog doesn't associate this movement with being called and thus anticipates the recall command) before uttering the word "Come", prefixed by the dog's name. That is, "Nell, come", spoken in a beguiling tone of voice.

If the dog doesn't respond, a light jerk on the lead is applied, and as the animal approaches the handler runs backwards for a few paces, all the while calling in an encouraging way. When the handler stops, and the dog is at hand, praise is lavish.

By tying a length of cord to the lead, and having the dog stay, the handler can move a fair distance away from the animal, yet still keep it under control. From 20 metres or so, the dog is recalled by the handler. If it is slow to respond physical compulsion is applied through the extra long lead. Once the dog is acquainted with the recall exercise with lead attached, it can be practised whilst the animal is running free.

In actual fact, it will most probably be familiar with returning to hand whilst running free anyway. From being a puppy, allowed loose in the garden or park, the walker or owner will have called the puppy's name and encouraged it to come to hand. More often than not it will have done so, particularly since it will have always been received with welcoming arms and generous words of warmth. Since this is so, formal obedience lessons might be superfluous. Indeed, one of the purposes of obedience whilst on the long lead as outlined is to reinforce the stay rather than recall. But the recall exercise is so vitally important, more especially for a blind person, that frequent and successful lessons are called for as an adjunct to routine dog training.

Occasionally, one meets up with the dog - good in other respects, more especially when confined to lead or harness - which is contumacious as far as the recall is concerned. What can the handler do in an effort to overcome this uncompliant animal? It is certainly useless to stand in the middle of a field and call endlessly to the dog in an effort to have it come to hand. By doing this, the animal learns more and more to ignore its master's voice. The handler should cease calling in a beguiling manner, and replace this tone with a threatening one. But only for a little while; it is better if response is to warm words rather than warning ones. The handler should try squatting on the ground, and calling the dog whilst positioned thusly. The dog is curious to see why its master has adopted this attitude, and runs across to see what it is all about. It becomes even more inquisitive if the handler lies prostrate on the grass - not very nice on a wet or snowy day - whilst calling the dog. This resort often brings even the most wayward dog smartly to hand. However, having approached the handler, the lead should be quickly affixed to the dog, since an animal of this uncomplying nature whilst running free will be adept at dodging aside and continuing its escapades should the owner be slow in confining it. The dog, of course, is praised once it is back on the lead.

A dog not answering the recall should not be pursued by the handler in an attempt to capture it. This action is doomed to failure. In actual fact, the opposite ploy should be used. The handler should walk away from the dog, as if to return home or to the training van or centre under his own steam. Such an action, of course, might be difficult for a blind person to employ, but nevertheless he should certainly try to make some way off in the opposite direction to the defiant dog. In case of such an unfortunate contingency, it is wise to keep in pocket or handbag the collapsible type of white symbol cane, to make one's way to the park gates or such. Paths criss-crossing parks can usually be easily followed. And sheepishly following its fast disappearing owner is often to be found the formerly recalcitrant dog.

Not to be forgotten as a prime inducement to effect a fast recall from a previously non-compliant dog is that useful device, the bribe. This is the only time a guide dog owner will resort to the use of food as a reward for his charge, since the animal is expected to work willingly through its own subservience as a lower member of the pack, and for the words of praise which ensue from its leader for tasks well done. But it is quite permissible, indeed to be encouraged if the desired results are forthcoming, to use a biscuit or two as an immediate reward for the wayward dog which eventually comes to hand in response to the recall. Once the dog realises that there is food to be had if it returns to hand, then its response to future commands "Come" will be all the quicker. If all else fails, the dog should never be allowed to run free.

The unfortunate habit of an over-friendly dog jumping up at people is to be discouraged. The puppy - walked dog will, with rare exceptions, have been broken of any such tendency whilst still in infancy, but where an adult animal is met up with which persists in rearing up to spread mud on an admirer's clothing, or snag stockings and tights, then these antics must be quelled. The therapy is short and sharp. As the dog jumps up, so an abrupt slap on the muzzle with the flat of the hand is given, together with a few harsh words. If the dog is insistent, then another slap is administered. It will not be too long before the dog discovers it is much more to its advantage if it greets a person by remaining on all fours, rather than attempting to literally bowl the individual over.

7

INDUCTION TRAINING

The pattern of training leading from induction of the raw dog to a class-standard animal commonly spans a period of four months, more or less, on a five-day working week basis and involving two training walks a day (one morning, one afternoon, but quite in order to adjust these walks to other times of the day, e.g., both sessions in the afternoon, but with a healthy break between; also, it is not imperative to stick rigidly to two walks per day. Perhaps once a day occasionally; perhaps thrice a day now and again) thus resulting in 10 walks a week, with a grand total of 160 walks (although the spaying operation and subsequent convalescence will lose perhaps two week's work, reducing the total to 140 walks) of approximately 40 minutes to one hour's duration each. So it will be seen that training a guide dog calls for a fair amount of stamina on the part of the trainer, especially when it is borne in mind that he will be handling, invariably, some five or six dogs concurrently.

The first three weeks of training is often combined, as we will discuss, with a testing and assessment period whereby it is finally decided by the trainer whether or not a dog will be suitable for acceptance. If otherwise, the dog is rejected and sold as a pet to a suitable owner offering a good home to the animal. Bear in mind, however, that the dog will already have been the subject of a preliminary assessment, in the home area, where the visiting trainer will have - albeit in a short space of time - tested the dog which is being offered for sale, or as a gift, to the organisation (see Chapter 5), whilst the puppy-walked dog will have been under the surveillance of the puppy-walking supervisor (see Chapter 3) and during this continuing evaluation will have been rejected earlier if undesirable characteristics evidence themselves. Since this initial weeding out will have taken place previously, the trainer may assume that the new batch of dogs under his jurisdiction will all be suitable candidates for guide dog training. In practice, however, one or two unsuitable animals still manage to show up

Not unnaturally, in the space of an hour or so spent in the home area of a dog offered for training, not all faults might come to light as far as canine temperament and ability are concerned, and the trainer returns in good faith to the training centre with the new dog in the expectation that it should make the grade; similarly, blemishes may go undetected in the puppy-walked dog by the puppy-walker and the puppy-walking supervisor. It is in these cases that the trainer, during the initial three week testing and assessment period which takes place during induction training, might detect a fault in a particular dog which renders it unsuitable for training. It might be acutely distracted by cats, for instance, which previous observation did not reveal to this degree, and which no amount of correction will counteract (with focus firmly fixed on a passing cat, canine body sensitivity may - on such an occasion, even in the instance of a normally sensitive dog - be lowered to the extent that verbal, let alone physical, admonition is ineffective); it might similarly be distracted by farm animals; it might be too 'hard' or too 'soft'; it might suddenly show aggressive tendencies towards strangers: for these and other latent, undiscovered or developing imperfections, the dog may have to be rejected.

So it is that for the first three weeks of training, the trainer will be especially observant with regard to the dog's reactions in particular situations and in potential areas of stress. Any negative tendencies exhibited by the canine - bearing in mind that in controlled cases further habituation may well overcome such failings (e.g., a dog slightly suspicious of heavy traffic may subsume this fear with sympathetic handling; an animal with scent or dog distraction could be corrected of these tendencies) - will be greeted by dubiety by the trainer, and if the faults persist or are patently ineradicable, then rejection will be the only answer. Of course, even at the termination of the three week testing and assessment period which introduces induction training, canine faults which have lain dormant may thereafter appear or develop, or a desirable positive trait may regress into a negative one, again rendering rejection inevitable. But this initial assessment should uncover all if not most canine faults (if any) and the guide dog trainer, having formally accepted the requisite number of desirable dogs, can now continue training with increasing confidence and earnestness.

The testing and assessment stint will have been undertaken in many differing conditions (bridges, subways, crowded school playgrounds, factories and offices, stairs, lifts, escalators, swing and revolving doors, railway stations, roads with heavy traffic, quiet country lanes with farm stock evident, sudden, loud noises, and all such manner of environmental features) and the accepted dogs, having been found equable in these situations, now begin a more formalised stage of training which deals primarily with the conditioning of the animal to the *straight line concept*. This consists of (with the dog, as always, on the left hand side of the trainer, walking slightly ahead - but not immediately in front - to the extent that the dog's hindquarters are almost brushing the left leg of the handler. As the dog forges ahead, the lead should be taut, so that the handler may comfortably follow without being pulled along) walking the dog along a lengthy stretch of wide, fairly quiet pavement, encouraging the dog to keep to the centre of the pathway (slightly right of centre is to be preferred to left, as we shall see later) and correcting the animal if it is distracted in any way. Each intersecting road is similarly crossed in a direct and unswerving path and, the up-kerb having been reached, the straight line concept over the ensuing stretch of pavement is continued.

The only exceptions to remaining in a straight line are when people and obstructions need to be avoided on the pavement, and an appropriate diversion made; similarly with parked cars (if any) at intersecting roads. The introduction of the straight line concept also paves the way for the initiation of three words of command and their requisite response.

At the commencement of a training walk the dog stands or sits motionless facing the direction of travel. If it tries to move or twist around the handler quickly compels it to remain static in the original position. The handler, standing adjacent to the right of the animal's hindquarters, imparts the command "Forward", and a flick of the lead at the same time encourages the dog to move off as requested. At this early stage of training only the lead with choke-chain is affixed to the dog; the harness has not yet been introduced.

The dog soon associates the stimulus of the word of command "Forward" with the action of moving smoothly and decisively straight ahead. Having reached the outward point of the journey so that the team is ready to return to the van or training centre, the command "Stop" is issued, accompanied by a jerk on the lead to compel the action. With association of word and deed, the injunction alone - spoken in these early stages in a most authoritative manner - suffices to impel the animal to halt.

To retrace steps, the handler remains stationary, with feet more or less together alongside the dog's seated or standing hindquarters and, as is the animal, facing the original direction of travel. He then imparts the sharp command "Back" and begins to retrace his steps whilst praising his charge for executing the turn.

The first two weeks of induction training (see Figure 7-1) can be concentrated upon the areas of straight line concept; the capturing of the dog's concentration, whilst working, by diligently, quickly and firmly correcting any inclination on the part of the canine to be distracted; and teaching the animal to respond promptly to the commands

"Forward", "Stop" and "Back". In addition, the socialisation of the dog continues by the handler having the animal indoors for lengthy periods both through the day and overnight. The dog is told to "Stay" in its bed whilst the handler leaves the room. He will surreptitiously listen for signs of ill-behaviour and movement and noise on the part of the dog whilst he waits outside, behind the closed door leading to the room wherein the animal is housed.

If noise or movement is detected within the room, the handler quickly and angrily barges in, and, verbally chastising the dog as he does so, forcibly and roughly replaces the animal in its bed, telling it again to "Stay". (The canine should not be praised when the trainer leaves the room; no words of warmth should be uttered. This might only serve to encourage the dog to follow the handler). This exercise is repeated at sporadic intervals until the dog may be left safely alone, for longer and longer periods, whilst it remains quietly in its bed. Upon return to the room after being away for a spell, the handler now praises the dog for behaving mutely and responsibly whilst on its own.

In the case of a recalcitrant dog which persists, even after repeated training sessions accompanied by justified and appropriate chastisement, in ill-behaviour by moving out of its basket and perhaps jumping on furniture and generally making a nuisance of itself when the handler is absent, it might be expedient to restrict the animal to its bed and the immediate locality by tethering it to a chain lead which should be fastened securely to a firm fixture close by. A stout, indoor kennel might even be worthy of consideration to restrict the movements of the dog which unremittingly takes the liberty of making itself at home, in the best armchair, whilst its owner is out.

As the socialising process continues, so does strict attention to the guide dog work out-of-doors, keeping as far as possible to the routine of two training walks, each of up to one hour's duration, daily for five days per week during the four months it takes to conclude training.

The induction period extends to about one month (see Figure 7-1). We have seen that for the first two weeks of this time stress has been laid upon instilling the canine with the straight line concept and a ready response to the commands "Forward", "Stop" and "Back". When uttering the commands, the handler should do so with clarity and incisiveness, rather than volume. A short, sharp word is far better than a shout, and ultimately more readily responded to by the dog. To begin with, the commands will need to be accompanied by physical compulsion before the stimulus of the injunctions themselves will be sufficient to evoke appropriate responses from the dog. Therefore, as (initially) the command "Forward" is issued, it will need to be accompanied by an outward flick of the lead, so that the movement is initiated by the handler himself. These movements and the command must be implemented simultaneously.

Figure 7-1

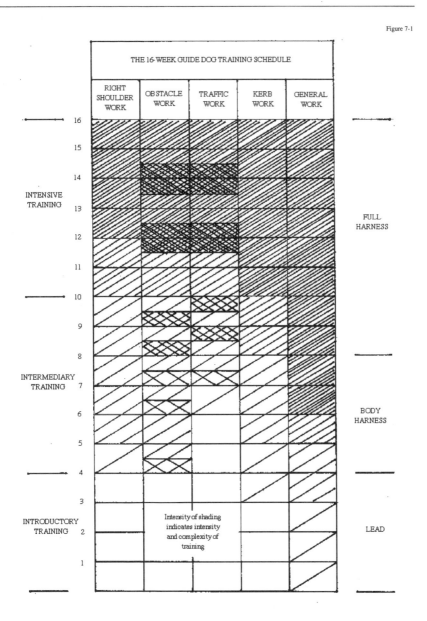

THE 16-WEEK GUIDE DOG TRAINING SCHEDULE

Intensity of shading indicates intensity and complexity of training

Before long, the dog will associate the injunction with the desired movement forward, and will respond accordingly. When this occurs, the handler should wait for tension to be taken up on the lead (which is slack whilst the unit is stationary) and as soon as the attachment tightens he should follow smoothly, and not wait to be pulled forward, which would probably stop the dog in its tracks.

On occasion, the dog, even when previously it has been responding readily to the command, may be paying attention to something else (which it should not) and consequently ignores the injunction. If this is so, the command should be instantly negatively reinforced by physical compulsion, by manipulating the lead forward so that the dog has no other choice but to move off. The movement serves the dual purpose of correcting the dog for being distracted, and a negative reinforcement to impel the desired action. The physical compulsion should be accompanied by another and more demanding verbal command "Forward".

The same principles apply to the commands "Back" and "Stop". When along a pavement where time deems it necessary to return to the vehicle which has been used to convey the dog, or to the training centre, the command "Stop" is imparted. At first, a jerk of the lead might be necessary (accompanied by the word of command) to halt the dog (to prevent the animal slewing round at an angle, an additional step forward so that he comes to a standstill alongside the dog's forequarters is taken by the handler) but before long the dog will respond to the verbal instruction alone.

A pause in time is allowed to elapse whilst the dog - which must stay sitting, or four feet planted firmly on the ground, in its original stopping place, and should be scolded and replaced if it tries to do otherwise - awaits the next instruction of the handler. The latter, by sliding first one foot and then the other backwards for one pace, reverts to his standing position alongside the dog's hindquarters, both feet more or less together, and from there issues a sharp command "Back".

Initially, a jerk backwards and to the right with the lead accompanies the command. Alternatively, a pat on the right thigh with the right hand may suffice as an accompaniment. However, it will not be too long before the dog responds to the verbal injunction alone, and moves, via the right of the handler (that is, it does a right about turn) to face in the direction from whence it came and, without pause, begins to retrace its steps. As this 180 degree movement is executed, the handler, turning neatly round on the spot in collusion and harmony with the dog, steps off smartly with the animal as it heads off on the return part of the journey.

As each command is satisfactorily responded to, then (needless to say) warm words of praise are issued. The words themselves may be meaningless and unrecognisable to the animal, so long as an endearing tone which is interpreted by the dog as a welcome, verbal reward is displayed by the handler, based on the popular impartations: "Good girl. There's a good dog then. What a clever girl." It is important that the words are spoken with feeling so that genuine warmth and delight is projected from the handler to the dog in such a way that the animal is markedly pleased to be the recipient of these delightful messages.

Should it be that the dog is so taken by these words of praise (the handler should avoid physically patting or caressing the animal, since this might only serve to encourage it to look towards and turn to face him, thus losing position and adversely affecting the work in hand) that it momentarily pauses in its stride, or alters its stance and looks up at the trainer, then he should modify his tone of voice to counteract this undesirable reaction. When the dog is mobile, working satisfactorily and concentrating well, such a desirable continuity should not be interrupted by outside influences; similarly, when it is static, it should not change its posture until commanded otherwise by the handler.

The simple body-harness fitment may be introduced about three or four weeks from the beginning of induction training. A couple of weeks later the handle can be affixed to the harness so that the complete guide dog accoutrement, the tangible guiding link between man and dog, is now being worn. However, the timing of the introduction of these fitments is arbitrary, give or take a week or so. Where the handle is a permanent attachment to the body-harness then of course the full fitment will be worn from the moment of inauguration.

Most dogs accept wearing the accoutrement with little disturbance. An occasional dog, usually of a high body sensitivity, may baulk a little at first at feeling this fresh fitment, but after one or two walks thinks nothing more of it. To be borne in mind by both handler and dog is the implication behind the donning of the harness. The equipage implies guide dog work from the moment it is put on until the time it is taken off. To countenance anything less demeans the work ethic associated with, whilst being worn, the guide dog harness. This ethic must be nurtured and preserved by the handler concerned, and impressed upon the dog through an appropriate mixture of negative and positive reinforcement as circumstances deem, during ensuing training.

The dimensions of the body-harness obviously depends upon the size of the dog (although the girth strap is adjustable), and the length of the handle is, as we shall discuss later, dependent upon the height of the dog and the height of the blind person to whom it is ultimately allocated.

In rare instances a dog may react against the introduction of the harness by adopting a 'crabbed' manner of walking; that is, it proceeds along with a slightly arched back and its hind legs angled inordinately outwards rather than immediately following the front legs in a straight line as normally they would. This action is aesthetically displeasing, and can be rather uncomfortable for a blind person to follow, but if all other things are equal the crab gait of such a canine can be lived with. Occasionally, the feature rights itself spontaneously. Conversely, where the fault becomes acute to the extent that the dog develops a severe left tendency whilst walking, rather than occupying the centre of the pavement and crossing roads in a straight line, it will merit rejection.

Too early an introduction to the harness-handle may result in this adverse reaction from the dog of a crabbed gait, since it now finds itself restricted in dimension of movement and consequently endeavours to increase its area of freedom by angling away to the left in an effort to escape from the confines of the harness and the dictates of the handler. By looping a long lead to embrace the left side of the dog the crabbed gait may be controlled somewhat, as will the attempts of the animal to move to the left. Often, however, the cure is only temporary, and when the lead returns to normal use the crabbed gait rears its ugly head again.

Rather than spend a lengthy period of potentially wasted training time in trying to right the fault, and bearing in mind the fact that these isolated dogs which assume such a peculiarity of gait seem also to be self-interested specimens, it is often as well to reject them. Happily, the overwhelming majority of guide dogs in training accept the introduction of harness and handle with equanimity and please the eye as, at a comfortable and consistent pace, they confidently lead the handler whilst maintaining a straight and presentable mobile posture in the centre of the pavement.

Stopping at the down-kerb

When the dog is responding adequately and promptly to the verbal commands "Forward", "Stop" and "Back", and now that the conditioning to the straight line concept is becoming a reality and the animal is concentrating (bearing in mind that there is little doubt corrections will still need to be administered for occasional lapses) as it should whilst it is out on training walks, we can now consider the stop at the down-kerb.

There is no great desperation to quickly and frequently institute the idea of stopping at the kerb edge. Indeed, in order to counteract the possibility of kerb-shyness (a tendency on the part of the dog to stop too far away from the kerb edge because it has been compelled by the trainer to stop at every down-kerb it comes to in much too short a space of time) it is as well to introduce the stop at the kerb in a leisurely and infrequent manner, so that gradually, over a matter of six or seven weeks or more, the dog is slowly but surely conditioned to halting at the down-kerb. Stopping at the kerb follows the principles of operant conditioning. The dog is positively reinforced (by way of verbal praise) when it halts at the kerb, but, later on when the animal is conditioned to the procedure and yet it transgresses and tries to overshoot the pavement edge (as it may do at odd intervals) then the canine suffers negative reinforcement by way of vocal chastisement and bodily correction with the lead.

In practice, the trainer, when he arrives at a down-kerb, smartly issues the command "Stop". The dog, having been previously trained to respond to this command, correspondingly stops. The conditioned stimulus of the command "Stop" elicits the appropriate conditioned response of the dog coming promptly to a stand-still. The trainer does not thereafter repeat this process of enforcement by uttering the command "Stop" at every successive down-kerb. He only institutes it at sporadic intervals; as time goes on, however, he will continue with the procedure at increasing albeit measured momentum.

We are two or three weeks into induction training before the stop at the kerb is introduced; that is, if verbal commands are now being responded to satisfactorily. Shortly, it may be that the dog will be incapacitated for a week or so while it is undergoing spaying (or castration if male) and subsequent convalescence (see Figure 7-1). There are no specific dates of demarcation for such surgery on the dog, and it may be that neutering takes place later on in training. Whenever it is, obviously there will be some set-back in training because of time lost, but it will be found that the animal in question will soon recover, both from the operation and, with the application of the trainer, its relevant standard of training.

It is therefore of little consequence if the routine of gradually introducing the stop at the kerb to the dog is suspended by the need to have the animal neutered, or indeed if it falls ill (or the trainer himself is indisposed or on a short holiday) for a little while at any time. No matter at what stage of training a short interruption takes place, an able and dedicated trainer should certainly find it within his capacity to make up a deficit of time so long as it does not exceed two weeks. Beyond that, unless the dog is of extraordinary mettle, it is doubtful if it could be made ready for team-training (sometimes referred to as class-training, i.e., the training of the blind person and guide dog together) unless previous instruction was prolonged to accommodate time lost beforehand.

Since training the dog to stop at the kerb is a relatively extended and unhurried procedure, absences from instruction do not affect the animal's acquired responses as it might with another aspect of training. It is feasible to plan in terms of 10 or 12 weeks of leisurely application of positive reinforcement before finally achieving, or requiring, the desired conditioned response of stopping at the kerb, let alone six or seven weeks. But to allow additional time for consolidation and for a consistent and unfailing response of stopping near to the edge of every down-kerb to be exhibited by the dog, it is as well to settle for the latter period of training expenditure.

The point arises as to which posture the dog should be obliged to adopt whilst stationary at the pavement edge. A dog which stands, rather than sits, at a down-kerb, is more relaxed and comfortable in itself, and also less vulnerable as far as damage to that important appendage, the tail, is concerned. A dog which sits at a down-kerb where crowds of pedestrians mill about risks having its tail trodden on, or run over by a pram or child's tricycle. Also, on a wet or snowy or icy day there are not many dogs which welcome sitting down in such conditions, perhaps for some time whilst waiting to cross a busy road. Furthermore, this would render the animal's rear needlessly damp, and perhaps muddy, when, by standing, a dry coat would remain. It makes more work for the guide dog owner when he returns home, towelling a damp dog which has been made even messier through having to sit at the kerb. True, some dogs are cute enough to sit only on their haunches in such conditions, but notwithstanding this, rear ends still get dirty. Even on a dry pavement, a dog can unavoidably sit in all sorts of rubbish which might litter the ground, such as other dog's dirt or urine, patches of mud or puddles, chewing gum and sticky sweets.

It is easier for the handler to position himself alongside a standing dog, and he also cannot now inadvertently tread on the animal's tail, as he might if it was sitting.

The standing dog also executes a smoother take-off for the road crossing, and is less likely to be poorly positioned in readiness for the command "Forward". Sometimes, the dog which sits at the down-kerb, as it responds to the injunction to move off, does so by lurching to the left rather than stepping off straight ahead as its standing counterpart invariably does. By lurching away from the handler in this way, the subsequent crossing might not be effected in a straight line. There is little doubt, then, of the merit in having the dog stand at the down-kerb rather than sit. Especially when one takes into account the fact that, where a dog is being made to sit at down-kerbs, because of the extra compulsion involved, rather than just a straightforward stop, the constraint and discomfort suffered by the animal may make it a little kerb-shy. That is, it may approach the kerb reluctantly, and stop short of it.

All this is not to say, however, that dogs which are trained to sit at the down-kerb inevitably suffer some adverse consequences as a result. Often enough, this is not so, and where repercussions do occur, they may not be insurmountable and matters right themselves with time and training, and a dog sitting nicely at the kerb, to some, presents a pretty picture. But the more utilitarian representation is of a dog standing, so long as it remains stoic and unmoving in that position until commanded otherwise.

As each day of training passes, slowly but markedly the stop at the kerb is gradually implemented, in these early stages at the behest of the trainer. He continues at unrelated intervals, and at occasional down-kerbs, to issue the injunction "Stop" so that the dog immediately responds and halts at the pavement edge. Whilst at the down-kerb, the dog is not allowed to alter its stance; it must remain there unmoving until the command "Forward" is issued, at which it proceeds steadily across the intersecting road to reach, and step onto, the up-kerb and resume the journey in a straight line along the continuation of the pavement.

At each down-kerb for which a stop has been made, the trainer dallies for varying intervals of time. If he stayed at every down-kerb for, say, 10 seconds, and then issued the command "Forward", it would not be too long before the dog, appreciating the lapse of time, began to move off in pre-emption of the trainer's injunction. Later on, when the dog is completely conditioned to stopping at the kerb of its own accord, there may be merit in the animal showing this precipitating initiative and starting off across a clear road without waiting for a command. In these early stages of the conditioning process, however, the dog must await the command of the trainer.

With momentum gathering as the weeks go by, the trainer is asking the dog to stop at more and more down-kerbs. It is not imperative that the animal stops right at the very edge of the kerb, although if the dog halts with its front paws just at the rim of the kerb-stone, so much the better. But a foot or so further back is of little consequence. Should the trainer give the command "Stop" a little late so that the dog's front feet are actually in the roadway, again, at this stage it is matterless.

However, before long it will be noted that the dog is showing signs of initiating the stop at the down-kerb of its own volition. Whereas, before, the conditioned stimulus for halting at the kerb edge was the verbal command "Stop" imparted by the trainer, we are now approaching the situation where the stimulus will be provided by the down-kerb itself. At this transitional stage there are therefore two stimuli encouraging the dog to stop at the kerb; the primary conditioned stimulus of the word of command "Stop", and the secondary conditioned stimulus of the kerb edge itself. Soon, as the conditioning stratagem is refined, the single and primary stimulus eliciting the conditioned response in the dog of stopping at the down-kerb, will be the kerb edge alone.

When this phase is reached - and we have taken a number of weeks to arrive at this point - the dog, as it becomes more conscious of the down-kerb in the offing, begins to slow down its pace of walking as it approaches the pavement edge. At this juncture, the trainer will need to introduce a measure of verbal encouragement to keep the dog going to the edge of the kerb, otherwise it might stop prematurely too far away from the down-kerb. A pleasant and excited tone of voice should do the trick - but not excessively, otherwise the dog might overshoot the kerb.

Later, when the dog is fully conditioned to stopping at the kerb, it does not matter how enthusiastic the handler is in his use of the voice, the animal will (or should) stop forthrightly when it arrives at the down-kerb. In fact, with the dog positioned at the pavement edge, in order to strengthen its steadiness there, the handler can intentionally move around and jostle the dog and talk nonsense to it (but not uttering, of course, the command "Forward" until such time as the handler wishes to proceed) but all the while making sure the dog stays - should it attempt to move untowardly - where it should at the down-kerb.

In relation to this, as the dog approaches the down-kerb and comes to a stand-still, the handler should occasionally deliberately stumble over the pavement edge (as might a blind person who is just beginning to learn to use a guide dog) but ensuring that the dog remains steadily at the rim of the kerb even if, in his pretended clumsiness, the trainer has pulled on the lead (or harness-handle) in order to support himself. Such training in kerb steadiness is of extreme importance when the fairly near future is taken into consideration, where the dog is to be used by a blind person who might not be as fluent or well-balanced as the trainer whilst handling the animal.

Crossing the road

From its stance at the down-kerb, the unit of man and dog must now discharge a straight and safe crossing so that it may reach the up-kerb opposite, and either continue directly on its way along the pavement, or, if desired, execute a turn after stepping up onto the footpath and stopping.

The onus for making the decision as to when it is safe to cross the road is placed upon the shoulders of the guide dog owner. Since this is the case, it is wise for the owner to go over roads at such protected places as pedestrian crossings, subways or footbridges. A guide dog using a regular route, with initial help and practice, will soon begin to identify and unfailingly arrive at these safe crossing points. Where such points do not exist, however, all crossings are to be made at road intersections, preferably from corner to corner (see Figure 7-2) but involving at least one of these features. This is done because cars are not allowed by law to park at road junctions, and therefore do not impede access to a straight crossing for the guide dog unit. Furthermore, at road junctions vehicles must, of necessity, slow down and indeed are sometimes obliged to stop before proceeding into the main thoroughfare. Thus, the slow moving traffic also makes it safer for the unit to cross at these specific spots where corners are involved

Figure 7-2

OFF-SET, RIGHT-ANGLED and ROUNDED CORNERS

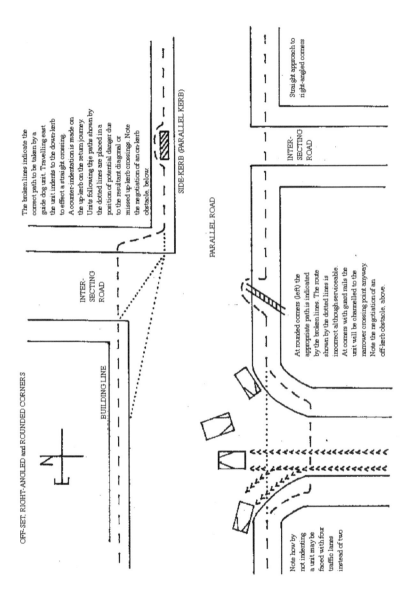

The broken lines indicate the correct path to be taken by a guide dog unit. Travelling east the unit indents to the down-kerb to effect a straight crossing.

A counter-indentation is made on the up-kerb on the return journey. Units following the paths shown by the dotted lines are placed in a position of potential danger due to the resultant diagonal or missed up-kerb crossings. Note the negotiation of an on-kerb obstacle, below.

SIDE-KERB (PARALLEL KERB)

INTER-SECTING ROAD

BUILDING LINE

PARALLEL ROAD

INTER-SECTING ROAD

Straight approach to right-angled corners

At rounded corners (left) the appropriate path is indicated by the broken lines. The route shown by the dotted lines is incorrect although serviceable. At corners with guard rails the unit will be channelled to the narrower crossing point anyway. Note the negotiation of an off-kerb obstacle, above.

Note how by not indenting a unit may be faced with four traffic lanes instead of two

85

Positioned at the down-kerb, both man and dog will now face toward the direction of travel; that is, looking across at the opposite up-kerb which is the point of access to head for. Although the dog may move its head from side to side, but without being distracted, in order to assess, both visually and aurally, the immediate traffic scene, it otherwise remains perfectly still.

The handler should be in alignment with the dog's hindquarters (whether the animal is standing or sitting) with the right foot - at the ready to take the first step as and when the dog responds to the command "Forward" - positioned a little behind the left, as if he had stopped in mid-pace. Indeed, in guide dog training parlance, this is known as the mid-pace position.

The general posture and stance of the unit gives an impression of relaxation and confidence. The person should not turn in towards the dog, or look down at it. He should face straight ahead, even when issuing commands. This is so that he might not inadvertently barge into the dog, or stand on its toes as it responds to his command "Forward" and moves across the road. If such a collision were severe enough, it might knock the dog off course and thus prove difficult for it to reach the up-kerb. However, it must be stressed that a good guide dog should be well able to withstand these buffets without altering course.

Having adopted the proper stance, the handler now prepares to issue the command "Forward". He waits a little while before so doing, and indeed varies the time spent at each down-kerb so that the dog is discouraged from anticipating words of command, which might be the case if injunctions were to be imparted at regular intervals. But the prime reason the handler does not promptly leave each down-kerb is so that he can afford the time to listen carefully for approaching traffic. Only when he feels the road to be clear does he give the word to move off to the dog.

If the command is ill-judged and uttered when vehicles are in dangerous proximity, as we shall discuss later when dealing with traffic work, the dog will respond to these moving cars by ignoring the command to go forward. The animal, however, is not infallible in this respect, which is why it is impressed upon the guide dog owner to listen with utmost caution before issuing the command "Forward".

The road being clear, the dog moves off. As it does so, as soon as he feels the animal begin to respond, the handler does likewise and steps smoothly off the kerb in unison with the dog. He does not allow tension to build up on the harness-handle, thus necessitating the dog pulling the person off the kerb, since this would result in distortion of unity, and ultimately the animal, because of the resistance offered it manually, might begin to hesitate upon the word of command "Forward", knowing it to be uncomfortable to respond to.

Once in the roadway, the unit proceeds steadily across the street in an unhurried manner. Notwithstanding having listened carefully at the down-kerb before giving the command, the handler may have missed the approach of traffic on the other side of the road, and in order for the dog to stop in response to the stimulus of these vehicles looming up on the far side of the street (see Chapter 8) the crossing must be made at a leisurely, albeit positive pace.

An unhurried crossing also gives the guide dog owner more time and indication to step onto the up-kerb without tripping, which could result from a too fast traverse. If the dog tries to cross too quickly, the handler should control the pace by introducing a monotonous drawl into his voice which imparts the need for slowness by its very tone: "Steady, girl. Steady, now. Steady," or words to that effect. The meaning is expressed by the descriptive vocal modulations rather than the actual words used.

If verbal intervention alone does not have the desired result, speed control can be physically effected (in conjunction with the vocal entreaties) by plying the harness-handle up and down in concert with each pace taken. The left arm, holding the harness-handle, is lifted slightly, to about mid-forearm height (the elbow - in contradiction to most other aspects of guide dog work, since a bent elbow is frowned upon in all other cases - pivots in order to allow this) and then the arm falls back into the correct position straight by the side.

This up-and-down movement, with practice, becomes a simple and fluid manoeuvre which assumes a rhythmic pattern as it is repeated with each step taken, and, dependent upon the severity of the fall-back of the arm, results in the dog walking at the pace which the handler deems. Of course, if the crossing is made too slowly, the handler must encourage the dog to move more quickly by talking to it in a bright and excitable tone of voice. The intention is a straight and definite crossing undertaken at a moderate, comfortable and controllable speed.

Turns

Directional turns in guide dog work are implemented simply by uttering the words of command "Left" or "Right" to the animal. Although most turns are made from the standing position at the down-kerb or up-kerb, an experienced guide dog owner can and does give directional commands to his equally well-versed charge whilst on the move.

To initiate turns in guide dog training, however, all such directional signals are given only when the handler has adopted the *hindquarter position*; that is, standing, in a relaxed manner, with both feet more or less together alongside the animal's hindquarters, and, as is the dog, facing straight ahead.

In order to turn right, the handler, as always with the dog on the left, and remaining in the hindquarter stance turns his face in the direction of intended travel (i.e. faces right) and issues a smart command "Right". The dog is told firmly to stay if it tries to move beforehand. It must await the directional command.

Obviously the dog is unaware of the meaning of the word to start with, so, to accompany the injunction, the trainer takes the lead in the free hand and jerks it briefly to the right at the same time as he gives the verbal command. Because of the physical compulsion through the lead, the dog has no choice but to move off to the right, and as it does so the handler steps off smartly with it in the new direction of travel, keeping to the correct walking position (alongside the dog's hindquarters with handle arm, as ever, by the side) as he does so. If the handler hangs back during this procedure, he may involuntarily fleetingly get behind the dog and thus unintentionally run the risk of treading on its hind toes.

The movement, as with all others in guide dog practice, must be smoothly executed, not only for the comfort of the animal but so that careful guiding can be implemented, and so that the unit looks aesthetically pleasing. Before long, the dog will be responding to the verbal directional command "Right" alone, and the use of the lead to effect a prompt response can be dispensed with.

The left turn, at first sight, and when first put into practice, appears a little more difficult to perfect. Again, the manoeuvre starts from the standing hindquarter position. The trainer issues the command "Left" and the dog responds by moving *right about* in front of the handler, who, circling on the spot, turns round smoothly with the dog, keeping the arm by the side, until a full three-quarter circle is completed, and the two now set off in their new direction of travel. As will be seen in Figure 7-3, the unit, originally facing - if we may use a clock dial to describe the movement - 12 o'clock, has now turned clockwise for 270 degrees to nine o'clock, upon which the team steps off smoothly on the changed route to the left. This circuitous method of turning left is employed in order to avoid a possible confrontation with a post should the handler simply turn into the intended direction of travel.

With practice, the left turn becomes a simple and smooth manoeuvre for both dog and man. To initiate it, however, the lead will need to be taken into the free hand to show the dog what is required. But in a comparatively short space of time, the lead need not be used and verbal command alone will suffice.

THE LEFT TURN

The dotted lines show the route
to be taken — via the right,
a threequarter circle is completed
before proceeding in a leftward
direction. Ample clearance is left
to avoid the lamp post.

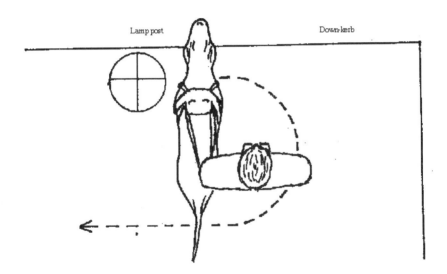

Lamp post   Down-kerb

8

ADVANCED TRAINING

Obstacle work

Whilst undergoing training, inevitably the team of dog and handler will come across obstacles of varying natures during their walks. The two commonest pavement obstructions are those provided by ladders (window cleaners, painters, slaters, etc.) and public service excavations (gas, electricity, telephones, water), and often the extent of these obstacles is such that it is necessary to leave the pathway in order to go round them. Scaffolding surrounding shops undergoing renovation is also commonly to be contended with, but usually in this situation there is sufficient clearance allowed for pedestrian access whilst remaining on the pavement.

Public service excavations, as well as openings to cellars, are commonly protected by barriers, and sometimes these fences channel pedestrians into a path on the roadway and subsequently back onto the pavement once the length of the obstacle has been negotiated. Because these obstructions are so clearly defined, the dog in training may, of its own initiative, make its way round the obstacle.

Should the dog attempt to go under one of the barriers however, it must be sharply stopped in its tracks with a decisive jerk of the lead or harness (bearing in mind body sensitivity), roundly scolded (bearing in mind hearing sensitivity), and the barrier slapped heartily with the right hand to attract the animal's attention, by way of this negative reinforcement, to the fact that it must not go under such encumbrances, but should rather go round them. The dog is then directed to its proper route around the obstacle.

The animal must of course stop at the down-kerb and await the command "Forward" before following the newly defined route offered by the public works excavators. The dog is encouraged to step back onto the pavement as soon as the obstacle has been negotiated, so that the unit remains in the road for the minimum amount of time. Verbal inducement is used, together with visual directional indications with the free arm to encourage the dog round the hindrance. Praise is forthcoming when the animal successfully overcomes the obstacle.

Where a single ladder straddles the pavement, the time spent in the road whilst going round this pedestrian impediment is minimal. However, because such ladders are less-clearly defined than the more distinct barriers, the dog might more readily go under them, thus introducing the possibility of the handler striking his head against the upper part of the structure. This, of course, underlines the urgency for good obstacle work in guide dog training; the need to protect the handler from harm.

Often, the dog will come across obstructions under which it could safely proceed, but in so doing it would place the handler on a collision course. On any occasion, therefore, when an obstacle presents itself and the dog is inclined to go under it, then the animal is brought smartly to a halt and admonished bluntly. Negative reinforcement is applied as the offending obstacle is banged and slapped with the free hand, so that this aversive therapy will discourage the dog from attempting to go under obstructions when next encountered; its reaction will be, or should be, to go round them instead.

To further consolidate obstacle work, artificial training at an intensive level is introduced. That is to say, along a quiet stretch of pavement the trainer places, at staggered intervals, a series of ladders, barriers, buckets, bins and similar paraphernalia so that the ensuing training walk with each of the dogs in his charge necessitates successful negotiation of these various obstructions before the perambulation is concluded. It may be that the trainer will traverse this artificial obstacle course with his dog two or three times before concluding the training session, which will extend in time to anything between 15 and 45 minutes. Some of the obstacles will straddle the pavement, necessitating negotiation by stepping into the roadway and regaining the sidewalk once safely round the obstruction. These *off-kerb obstacles* can prove more difficult to contend with than the *on-kerb obstacles*, which can be rounded without leaving the pavement.

When obstacles are being negotiated, care is also needed on the part of the dog in that ample clearance must not only be left for the head height of a handler of some two metres tall (therefore overhanging impedimenta - shop awnings, tree branches, etc. – are additionally to be avoided, as reinforced by aversive therapy, i.e., banging and shaking the offending obstacle, thus attracting the dog's attention to it and the necessity for skirting it, by simultaneously scolding the dog verbally, and physically by mildly slapping its muzzle, dependent upon canine sensitivity, and pushing the animal to one side to emphasise the urgency for obstacle elusion) but furthermore, when the obstruction is to the right of the unit, then a wide enough gangway must be allowed by the dog for the handler on its left, so that the latter does not collide with the obtrusion.

An artificial obstacle course may consist of some seven or eight obstructions spaced along a 200-metre stretch of pavement, perhaps with a couple of intersecting road crossings along the way. In order to strengthen positive responses from the dog when confronted with obstructions, three or four days of concentrated artificial obstacle training might be indulged in each alternate week during, say, a six-week period (see Figure 7-1).

The trainer must carefully measure the dog's acceptance of, and response to, obstructions, however, since it may be that, where stints of obstacle work become too intensive for a particular dog, the animal may react adversely. It may become unwilling, for instance, and it may anticipate obstacle avoidance to the extent where it begins to stop some few metres away from the barrier to be negotiated, rather than approaching close to it. If a guide dog user were to give the command "Forward" when his dog was at a standstill some fair distance away from the obstacle, then the unit would be spending a great deal of unnecessary time travelling off the pavement, and perhaps exposing both man and dog to danger from passing traffic, when ideally the barrier should be rounded promptly with the minimum of dalliance in the road.

To counter a tendency on the dog's part to display obstacle shyness, the trainer will need to resort to a surfeit of positive reinforcement. Verbal expressions of joy and delight, jangling the lead gaily, and skipping with the dog when it shows a reluctance to approach an obstacle should help to keep it plodding on so that it stops, as it should, close to the obstruction.

The situation and nature of the structures should be changed from day to day during artificial obstacle training sessions. If the same obstacles were left in the same position each day without change, because of a dog's failure to discriminate it may be found that it is beginning to respond to the site whereon the obstacle is positioned on the pavement, rather than the obstacle itself. That is to say, even if the barrier were to be removed, the dog might still avoid the place on the pavement where it previously stood. Positive reinforcement will, however, soon overcome this, which anyway only occurs with isolated dogs which might be lacking a little in initiative and perception and, additionally, are often on the sensitive side. Nevertheless, instances such as this serve to underline the need to alter the shape of the obstructions themselves, as well as the sites they occupy, during intensive artificial obstacle work. Furthermore, obstacle training must be practised both with the parallel road on the right, and on the left.

Ideally, obstacle observance on the part of the dog should be both spontaneous and neat. In essence, once artificial obstacle training sessions have been successfully concluded, the transition to natural obstacle avoidance should be smooth and effective. To help achieve this, natural obstructions met up with during the course of the regular routine training walks before, after and during artificial obstacle work, can do nothing but good. In this way the dog begins to appreciate real obstacles in the real world. To further help in this direction, it is not a bad idea for the trainer to have readily at hand a collapsible type obstacle which he can erect where-ever he feels practical on a spot along the route he is about to undertake with his dogs. These one-off obstacles, appearing as they do without prior warning (unlike the more unreal and 'cued' atmosphere of the intensive, artificial training course) make the dog more aware of the need to be vigilant whilst working in harness, and be prepared to contend with the unexpected, such as the sudden appearance of an obstruction along a previously unimpeded path.

It is not unprecedented for an impasse to be presented insofar as natural obstacles are concerned. It may be that the unit has been channelled into a dead-end, without access to left or right and faced with an impassable obstruction. All the team can do is retrace steps and seek an alternative avenue of escape. Isolated instances such as this are seldom encountered, however. Most obstacles conventionally allow for the minimum of negotiation, now that public works contractors and others are becoming more aware of the need to take appropriate safety precautions when obstructions are perforce erected.

A not unknown situation which indicates an impasse - although, barrier notwithstanding, satisfactory negotiation can still ensue - is where an obstruction blocks a pavement and a car has been parked so close to it that it is impossible for the unit to proceed further forward, or to deviate left or right (depending upon which side the parallel road is). If the parallel road is on the right, then the dog, when faced with the obstacle, must swing right about the handler (who, keeping to the correct position alongside the dog, arm by the side and handle loosely held in the up-turned fingers of the left hand, follows smoothly) and retraces steps (the parked car is now on the left) until the opening into the road at the end of the car's length presents itself, whereupon the dog veers to the down-kerb and stops. From here, upon the word of command "Forward", it goes round both car and obstacle and promptly regains the pavement once past the two impedimenta.

When the side road is on the left and a similar situation of obstacle with parked car alongside presents itself, the dog again swings right about but, having gone the length of the standing vehicle, now deviates right to halt at the down-kerb of the parallel road, where, at the command "Forward", obstacle (including car) negotiation ensues.

Most obstructions contended with in everyday guide dog activities are, however, on-kerb obstacles. As the name implies, the nature of these obstructions is such that they do not necessitate leaving the path. And in fact, so readily are they dealt with by the dog that the guide dog user is often unaware of the fact that negotiation has been safely and discreetly accomplished.

Pavement impedimenta involving on-kerb obstacle avoidance include half-barriers erected by contractors involved in excavation work (with wide enough unobstructed access left for both man and dog), ladders straddling only partly across the pathway, dustbins, children's tricycles left temporarily unattended, and other familiar sidewalk clutter.

The dog must be trained to go smoothly round the common paraphernalia which litters the modern urban pavement, but additionally must be encouraged to do so, whenever practicable, and where-ever access is wide enough, by placing itself between the object and the handler. In this way, less danger presents itself to the handler's right. Therefore, if a dustbin is in the centre of the pavement, the dog should go to the right of it in order to pass it by. Obviously, where a dustbin is too far to the right on the pavement in the face of the oncoming unit, so that the narrowed access on the right prohibits a safe and wide enough pathway for both man and dog to pass, then the dog will need to move to the left in order to get round the receptacle. In so doing, however, as we shall discuss in the section on right shoulder work, due allowance must be made by the dog for the width of the handler, thus enabling safe passage without him colliding into the dustbin.

Right Shoulder work

A high standard, bordering on the infallible, of *right shoulder work* is essential in guide dog training so that the blind handler will be free of the stress that accompanies mobility when his thoughts might be occupied with the possible danger of collision with a solid object, be it static or moving. The constant fear of such unwelcome contact accounts for the poor posture and trepidation whilst travelling alone on foot of a number of blind people. In this respect, a good guide dog not only sets its handler's mind at rest, but at the same time encourages an improvement in posture and a more relaxed stance.

The onus is upon the trainer to effect right shoulder work to its maximum potential as far as response from the dog is concerned. By right shoulder work we mean the capacity of the dog to leave ample room for the handler on its right when it is going round lamp standards, parking meters, sign posts, traffic lights and all similar street furniture that beset our pavements in this present day, to the ultimate extent that the guide dog user unfailingly avoids collision with these inanimate objects.

But what of animate objects? By the same token, these also, the pedestrians on a busy pavement, are to be scrupulously avoided to ensure a safe course for the handler. Closely akin to right shoulder work (right shoulder is a synonym, indicating the dog's propensity to protect the total front of the person, from head to toe, who walks at its right side), which is why we deal here with both aspects together, is this area of training dealing with avoidance of fellow foot travellers which we describe as *crowd work*. Pedestrians in groups or singly, mobile or static, moving in a variety of directions at a variety of speeds, mothers pushing prams, invalids in wheelchairs, children on tricycles or roller skates, all must be kept at that distance which allows safe transit for the handler.

Right shoulder work can be introduced into the routine almost from the outset of training, and it is a continuing process. To begin with, as the dog is walking along the pavement during the course of a training walk, and the trainer finds that he will be in dangerous proximity to a lamp post which the two are fast approaching, then when he is almost upon the fixture he should flick the lead to the left and admonish the dog as he indicates the post with his right hand.

As time and training goes on, right shoulder work becomes more intense. Depending upon response from the dog, together with its degree of sensitivity, the reinforcement of right shoulder work and crowd work by the trainer increases in severity. If the dog does not allow enough leeway, for instance, whilst rounding a post or person, the dog is verbally admonished as (now that it is probably working in harness) a left-ward flick administered on the harness-handle pushes the dog over somewhat in the requisite direction. A fairly forceful nudge with the left knee (takes practice for the trainer to become quick and adept at this without stumbling over or losing pace) and a rapid tattoo on the offending post with the right hand helps to draw the more recalcitrant dog's attention to the error of its ways. All of this, of course, is effected without falter whilst the unit is wending its way along the pavement. The aim being for the dog to deviate accordingly whilst rounding an object, and then regain its walking position in the centre of the pavement. Each adequate deviation on the dog's part is rewarded with praise.

Where possible, the dog should deviate to the right. That is to say, where there is space enough on the right, the dog should put itself between the object or person being passed. However, if there is not enough room on the right, then obviously the animal must move over to the left and leave the requisite leeway for safe passage of the handler. With a crowd of pedestrians thronging the pavement, and without sufficient room to pass either side, the dog must stop and await a gap in the multitude of people before proceeding. On such occasions, the handler, standing correctly alongside the dog, can now and then mutter "Hup, hup. Hup, hup", to the animal so that it is reminded to progress along its way as soon as the opportunity presents itself.

As time goes on, the dog will develop its initiative with regard to crowd work and - allied with judicious handling techniques – should become adept in this important area of guide dog practice. For instance, where a gap is evident through a crowd of people, but is too narrow for safe access for the full width of the unit, an experienced guide dog will head for the breach and - still walking forward - will 'lean' on the person or persons to its left, thus obliging them to move further to the left and so leaving a gap wide enough for dog and handler to proceed through. If, however, a collision occurs with a pedestrian, the dog must be admonished, notwithstanding the fact that the force of the impact will serve some merit by way of unwitting negative reinforcement, since the shock waves, although of greater surprise and dismay to the two humans involved, will nevertheless fortuitously create some alarm in the animal.

On occasion in guide dog usage a total impasse may present itself. Except for a narrow gap, wide enough for only one person at a time to go through, the pavement and road alongside might be completely blocked by obstructions and excavations (right shoulder work obviously also applies to holes in the ground: the dog must allow more than ample room for its handler when trenches are being circumnavigated. Happily, public works excavations these days are - or should be - amply protected by encircling barriers) and in such an event the dog stops forthrightly at this slight opening. Even when the handler says "Forward" the dog quite rightly refuses to go.

In a rare instance such as this, the *narrow gap procedure* is employed to counter the situation. The handler rests the harness-handle on the dog's back (this is an indication to the dog that it is now not working as it normally would be) and, retaining the lead at its fullest extent in the left hand, the person positions himself - on this one occasion - immediately *behind* the animal. He now urges the dog to go forward. The animal might at first be hesitant, and certainly it should be encouraged to proceed only at a slow pace. The handler walks warily behind, following the dog (taking care not to tread on its hind paws) carefully whilst holding the lead, but as soon as the narrow gap is negotiated he takes up the harness-handle, readopts the orthodox stance and position of the guide dog user, and continues on his way.

Traffic Work

Once the dog is stopping consistently at the down-kerb, and responding promptly to the command "Forward", it is opportune to implement traffic training at intermittent intervals. At the occasional down-kerb, when a car or other vehicle, or number of vehicles, is approaching and it is obviously unwise or unrealistic to cross the road without endangering man and beast, the trainer issues the command "Forward". The dog, responding to the injunction and attempting to go across the road in front of moving traffic, is prevented from so doing by a slight jerk backward on the harness handle and a verbal expletive, "No, bad dog". A raised right arm indicates the approaching vehicle, by this time in close proximity to the unit, to the animal. Now the handler repeats quietly to the dog, "Hup, hup. Hup, hup", whilst restraining the animal physically, and verbally, should it show an inclination to move from the down-kerb. However, once the vehicle or vehicles have all filtered into the main road thus leaving the intersecting street clear, the dog may be permitted to respond to the trainer's reminders of "Hup, hup. Hup, hup", and cross over.

Having been stopped initially from responding to the command "Forward", and thereafter prevented from leaving the down-kerb until all traffic had gone, the dog may be a little unsure of what to do next, in which case the trainer may have to prudently encourage the dog to move by increasing pronouncedly the intensity of his verbal entreaties or, failing that, a slight upward and forward jerk on the harness-handle. Once the dog begins to cross the clear road, praise from the trainer ensues.

The traffic training discussed thus far is known as *near traffic*, where the dog must not leave the down-kerb because of vehicles immediately in front of it, moving from right to left (in countries where traffic drives on the right, the vehicular flow will be left to right). However, half-way across the road, *far traffic* (traffic moving from left to right) might appear, in which case the trainer will need to stop the dog with a downward and backward jerk on the handle (there is no command "Stop"; the stimulus for this response must be the moving car) and a gesticulation of the right arm indicating the advancing vehicle wherefrom there is no safe passage, because of lack of time and proximity of the motor, to move across in front of the offending object. The dog is therefore trained to stop and allow the vehicle to proceed along the road without falter. (Figure 8-1)

Figure 8-1

THE VARIED APPROACHES OF TRAFFIC

Broken lines and arrows show unit's direction of travel. (S) indicates the spot at which it stops. Projected path of vehicles is shown by dotted lines. The dog appreciates the intended line of travel of the approaching vehicle and stops accordingly even through the car is some distance away. But, bearing in mind vehicular speed the car could be upon the unit before it had crossed the road, thus being exposed to risk if a stop is not made. (Note, examples shown are for traffic being driven on left.)

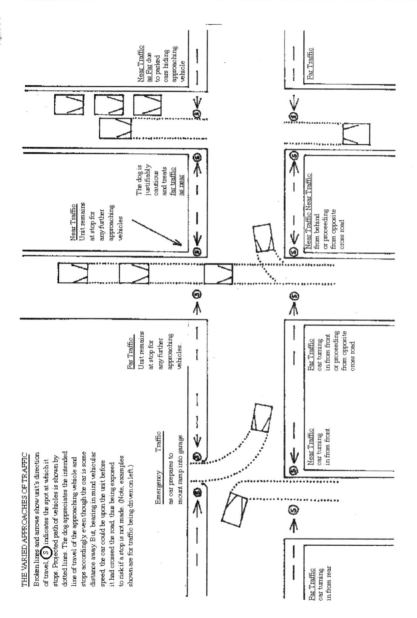

Near Traffic as Far due to parked cars hiding approaching vehicle

Far Traffic

Near Traffic
Unit remains at stop for any further approaching vehicles

The dog is justifiably cautious and treats far traffic as near

Near Traffic Near Traffic
from behind or proceeding from opposite cross road

Far Traffic
Unit remains at stop for any further approaching vehicles.

Far Traffic
car turning in from front or proceeding from opposite cross road

Near Traffic
car turning in from front

Emergency Traffic
as car prepares to mount ramp into garage

Far Traffic
car turning in from rear

Whilst stationary in the middle of the road, the trainer again says to the dog, "Hup, hup. Hup, hup", and encourages the animal to continue across the road once it is clear to do so. All roads must be crossed in a straight line. The dog must wait for moving vehicles to go away and the road be clear before crossing.

Only in rare instances or pressing circumstances, such as traffic jams or long queues of cars at particularly busy road junctions, would the dog be allowed to deviate around, or between (where there is space to do so) vehicles, during a street crossing. A source of concern to the dog when proceeding between or behind vehicles with their engines ticking over is of course the exhaust emission, which regrettably is often at the animal's head height. To allow some margin between these hot and obnoxious fumes, access between cars should be wider than might usually be expected.

The dog is of course permitted to make a detour round a car when it is broken-down, or parked at a road junction, even though the vehicle should not be lodged in such a dangerous spot. This is one of the compelling reasons why guide dog units, for the most part, should cross only at road junctions, since it is improper, as well as illegal, for motorists to park in these places.

The onus is ultimately upon the guide dog owner to take the initiative in crossing roads safely, because in these days of high-density traffic and fast-flowing vehicles on wide highways it is beyond the bounds of possibility for a dog, no matter how well-trained, to undertake such adventures without fear of accident. If, therefore, the guide dog owner is unsure about crossing a road, he should seek sighted assistance. A sighted individual helping a guide dog owner to cross a road should position himself to the right of the blind person, away from the dog. The blind person should take the sighted escort's left arm and rest the harness-handle on the dog's back, but still retaining the lead, and follow his companion smoothly when he moves off, telling his guide dog to "Come on, Nell". The escort should make certain the road is clear before crossing, and should tell the blind person when to step down or step up, as the case may be.

Much emphasis is consequently laid upon traffic work in guide dog training because of the potential dangers facing the blind person when beset with a busy road crossing. So although the safety of the unit eventually rests upon the guide dog owner, traffic work involving the training of the dog continues unabated, since it may happen that an ill-judged word of command "Forward" is not responded to by the animal on an occasion when it would be dangerous to cross a road. Or perhaps the dog stops promptly in the roadway when far traffic unexpectedly appears.

The induction of traffic work is slow and gentle, using natural traffic in the initial stages, and taking place during each training walk as and when opportune moments present themselves. The intensity, however, builds up over the weeks, and more comes to be expected of the dog, to the extent that negative reinforcement will be forceful (bearing in mind the sensitivity of the dog) should it respond to the command "Forward" when it is dangerous to do so, or fails to stop for far traffic.

About six weeks (see Figure 7-1) before over-all training is concluded immediately prior to allocation to a blind person, *artificial traffic work* is introduced to further induce the dog to act cautiously when cars are flying about. A training colleague, using a guide dog school car, drives along a series of intersecting roads in which vicinity his comrade is training his dogs. As each down-kerb is reached and the dog halts, the trainer gives the command "Forward" and at that crucial point the car, which is already proceeding along the road, has now reached the juncture where it would be unsafe for a pedestrian to cross, and, should the dog attempt to move off, it is corrected by the handler. If it ignores the command, it is praised. When the car has gone, the unit crosses the road.

Perhaps the 'artificial' car is used as far traffic, in which case the dog must stop, or is compelled to stop, in the middle of the road, to wait there until the vehicle has passed by. Whether for near traffic or far traffic, if the dog does not stay where it is when it should until the road is clear, and ignoring the handler's words in the meanwhile, negative reinforcement would not go amiss. The car driver can rev violently if he sees the dog try to move, and place the car in close proximity to the unit as he drives past, and the trainer can emphatically bang the side of the vehicle with the flat of his hand as it slowly passes by, and then perhaps slapping the dog's nose as he verbally admonishes the animal.

An unruffled departure from the down-kerb and smooth passage across the road is important once the car has gone. To allow the dog the opportunity to stop promptly for far traffic, road crossings should not be rushed. A steady progress is maintained across the road, not too slowly, and certainly not too quickly. Praise is issued when the dog proceeds unhurriedly. In addition to near and far traffic, garage run-ins and drive-ways extending across the pavement are used by the artificial vehicle to impress upon the dog the need to instantly halt should a car, driven by a mindless motorist who is not looking about him, descend suddenly from or into these entrances and exits, as so often they do.

Such sessions of artificial traffic training can be quite intensive, depending upon the responses from each individual dog. The usual format (see Figure 7-1) is a three-day traffic training stint of periods of about half-an-hour per day, morning or afternoon. Then an interval of about a week, during which routine training continues, followed by another three-day stint, after which, for dogs which are slow to respond, further artificial traffic work following a similar pattern until the desired canine performance is forthcoming. All the while, of course, *natural traffic work* - same principles and techniques as in artificial training, but this time involving all varieties of vehicles (including bicycles and motor cycles) which happen to be passing by whilst the unit is at a down-kerb - is taking place during the everyday training walks.

Just as roads do not follow a regular pattern, neither does traffic flow. Consequently, both artificially and naturally, the dog continues traffic training to the extent where it now begins to appreciate and respond to vehicles coming at it from all directions, as shown in Figure 8-1. Traffic turning in and out of road junctions, approaching from both behind and in front, must all be summarily dealt with by the dog. Traffic of this nature, as in its other aspects, is reinforced firstly through the artificial sector. But it is not too long before the dog is beginning to respond as adequately as one would hope for to natural as well as artificial traffic.

Further ramifications of traffic work involve those areas where we see *near traffic as far* and *far traffic as near*. It may be that the unit has left the kerb to cross the road, and a vehicle parked further along the street has left the dog unsighted. But having moved from the down-kerb, a car on the near-side now appears into view from behind the parked vehicle. The dog must then stop (see Figure 8-1). This is near traffic as far.

Far traffic as near we take as an indication that the dog is extra cautious. Upon the word of command "Forward", notwithstanding the fact that the near-side of the road is clear of traffic, the dog detects a vehicle or vehicles approaching along the opposite side of the road, and rather than proceed into the middle of the highway to make a stop, the animal ignores the injunction and remains where it is. Since the down-kerb is a much safer place than the middle of the road when traffic is passing by on the far side, this practice on the part of the dog is to be praised rather than frowned upon.

* * * *

Physiologically, the canine visual apparatus is much the same as in man. Light passes through the transparent cornea of the spherical-shaped eye, on through the anterior chamber, then the lens and vitreous body, ending up at the retina at the back of the globe. Changes occur in the cells of the retina under the stimulation of light, sending variable electrical impulses along the optic nerve to the brain, where the 'picture' is deciphered.

In dull conditions, to allow more light into the eye, the iris diaphragm surrounding the lens constricts to allow the passage of more light. On bright days, to protect the photo-sensitive cells of the retina from over-exposure, the iris expands to limit the entry of light by concealing the periphery of the lens, leaving only a small aperture at the front.

This action of the adaptable iris is an example of an unconditioned reflex. Upon the stimulus of bright light, the iris constricts, whereas on dull days it expands. The animal concerned has no control over the constriction and expansion of the diaphragm. The lens itself is pliable, and to change focus for different viewing distances the surrounding muscles flex this part of the eye accordingly.

By pathological examination of the canine eye, it seems that the range of focus is poor compared to that of man. This would appear to indicate that the dog views the external world slightly out of focus. The picture is not as sharp and clearly defined as it is for man.

The retina comprises two sets of light sensitive cells, the rods and cones, which names give some indication of their shape. The rods are responsible for visual reception under poor light, whilst the cones are concerned with colour, as well as day-time perception. Compared to man, the dog has many more rods and fewer cones throughout the retinal cells of the eye. This would account for the capacity of the dog to see quite well in the dark. The paucity of cones, however, would lead us to believe that the dog is colour-blind

More important than a sharp visual image for the dog, and something it pays more attention to, is movement. A dog looking out for its master from a distance will not recognise him as such when he is standing still, but when the owner begins to move it will identify him readily by his gait and stature whilst so mobile. An interesting experiment is for the owner, many metres away, to deliberately affect a strange gait and posture, and he will find that the dog is unable to identify him until he is near at hand (the owner will of course be down-wind of the dog) at which the animal may first recognise him by smell rather than sight.

Also lacking somewhat in the dog is the three dimensional capacity of sight which is evident in man. Stereoscopic vision such as this, which gives a depth of focus so that the object in view can be ascertained as being near or far away with some degree of accuracy, is limited - albeit not absent - in the canine when compared to man.

To sum up the visual scope of the dog, the depth of vision, ability to focus and differentiate static form is weak, it is colour-blind but has good night-time perception and rapid appreciation of movement. The dog is well able to accept these relatively minor visual imperfections, particularly when canine hearing and sense of smell are so acute.

*   *   *   *

Canine aural reception, which is on a par with its human counterpart on the low frequency ranges, far exceeds man on high level frequencies. Shrill noise (e.g., that emitted by bats and 'silent' dog whistles) which man is unable to detect, is perfectly perceptible by the dog. The upper limit of canine hearing extends to 30,000 cycles per second, whilst man falls short at the 20,000 cycles range.

The dog not only hears acutely well, but its ability to place sound, its capacity for such localisation, is estimated at twice the accuracy of man. This helps explain the guide dog's facility to deal with moving traffic safely when seemingly taking no notice of it. A guide dog does not rely upon sight alone when it responds to the stimulus of nearby traffic and so ignores the command "Forward". Often, it can be noted that the dog disregards the injunction to move off even though it is not visually taking note of approaching vehicles; in fact, it is looking the other way. This underlines the prepotency of the animal to rely upon its hearing to respond to traffic, to the extent where it aurally localises the vehicles and in so doing appears to assess a margin of safety whereby it is either safe to cross the road, or more prudent to stay with its handler at the down-kerb.

9

CONTINGENCY TRAINING

In view of the very nature of its duties, a guide dog should be accomplished in contending with the multifarious situations which it might encounter during the daily routine. Travelling on public transport, for instance. Whilst waiting at a bus stop, the unit is at the 'rest' position, where dog and man are stationary and the harness-handle lies on the back of the animal, which may stand or sit patiently at its owner's side who, of course, retains the lead. When a bus pulls up at the stop, if the entrance is wide enough the user picks up the handle and tells the dog to "Get on the bus". Should the entrance be narrow, the handler must use only the lead when following the dog onto the vehicle (see *narrow gap procedure*). Once on the bus, the dog is shown by the trainer to find the nearest vacant place (later, the dog itself is encouraged to "Find the seat"), whereupon the animal goes under the seat and lies on the floor.

It is best if the dog lies facing the aisle, otherwise it runs the risk of having its tail trodden on if this appendage projects into the gangway. Floors on buses can be pretty dirty, so in the interests of preservation and cleanliness of the harness, it is as well to remove the accoutrement. Also, it is more comfortable for the dog, as well as sustaining the 'work ethic' which the animal associates with the harness. But if it is only a short journey, and the handle is detachable, this only need be removed. As an alternative to lying on the floor, the dog can sit facing the handler, between his legs.

Tube and railway stations should be included in the guide dog's repertoire. When walking along a station platform, needless to say ample clearance must be allowed on the dog's right for safe passage of the handler. In fact, it is sound policy on the station concourse to have the dog well to the left so that the animal is nearest the platform edge.

When the train comes in, the dog is told "Get on the train" and, since tube and railway train carriages usually have doors wide enough, the handle may be retained to enter the compartment and the dog is told to "Find the seat". Once on the train, man and dog make themselves comfortable; often enough, on a crowded tube train, both will have to stand.

It will be appreciated that because of the many variations in construction and layout of public conveyances, innovation and adaptation will need to be employed by the handler for entering and leaving such a wide range of vehicles, and for positioning self and dog once aboard. It is important when entering a train that the handler makes due allowance for a possible gap between the platform and the carriage in case it is wider than average. Upon leaving the train, if other passengers haven't already disembarked, thus identifying the side whereon the platform is situated, then the guide dog owner must make sure the dog leaves first before stepping off. This measure precludes the handler (if he were to make the mistake of preceding the animal) leaving the carriage, disastrously, on the wrong side, since the dog will rightly jib at moving forward into empty space . Because of the width of gap between train and platform, and the depth of steps on the carriage, it may be necessary to use the long lead rather than the handle when getting the dog to go first on leaving the train.

To deal with flights of steps, the dog stops at the top and awaits the command "Forward". The animal then proceeds slowly downwards, the handler keeping to the correct position as he follows carefully. Because it is found to be awkward and indirect when trying to go up and down steps whilst holding the handle, it can be advantageous to both dog and man if the lead only is retained, but this is a question of personal choice which can only be resolved with practice. When faced with flights of steps upwards, the dog stops at the bottom with its two front paws on the first step. The handler puts his left foot on the first step and then gives the command "Forward". Where there is a hand-rail alongside flights of steps the less-steady person may wish to make use of it whilst proceeding up, or down, stairs with his dog.

The dog must be trained to enter and promenade safely around shops, stores and other buildings; if escalators are used the animal will need to be carried. With the left arm under the dog's neck, and the right arm cradling the rear part of the animal, with tail tucked underneath, the dog is carried onto the moving staircase. Where-ever possible, however, an alternative to the escalator is used. There are usually lifts and stairs that can be used instead.

When going into a restaurant, the more inconspicuous the dog the better; upon entering the establishment the animal is told to "Find a chair", and once this objective is reached, the dog immediately settles itself under the table where it remains quietly lying down, the harness having been removed, until such time as the handler is ready to leave.

Inevitably, there will be environmental circumstances unique to a particular guide dog user which will not have been covered during training, but a temperamentally sound and sagacious animal will soon be encouraged by the conscientious owner to do the right thing to suit particular situations. Common sense, and parallels in previous aspects of training, are all that are needed to achieve a successful outcome when dealing with a strange contingency.

Country roads without pavements

Why is it that the Highway Code recommends that pedestrians, when walking along roads without pavements, should travel on that side of the highway whereby they face oncoming vehicles? That is, where traffic drives on the left, pedestrians should proceed on the right. The answer of course is so that they will *see* traffic approaching them and, if the on-coming vehicle (because of a demonic or drunken driver) does not allow sufficient clearance for pedestrians, then the latter can take evasive action. The supposition is that, if pedestrians had their backs to the traffic, and consequently couldn't *see* it approaching, then there was an obvious danger of them being hit.

The operative sensory mechanism which is called into play in order to effect this road safety exercise is that of sight. But we are concerned here with blind people. Therefore, in this instance, the Highway Code instructions are rendered somewhat invalid. It really doesn't matter very much on which side of the road a blind person walks, so long as he keeps well into the side and as soon as he hears a vehicle (no matter whether approaching from front or behind, and anyway the blind person might not be able to differentiate this) he must stop and take some form of evasive action. This might involve stepping onto a grass verge, or keeping well into a hedge, or at least getting as far into the side of the road as possible. Whilst it is appreciated that most motorists are considerate folk, self-protection by pedestrians must be taken on roads without pavements because of the occasional incapable or inconsiderate driver.

When walking along a country road without pavements, the blind person should try to ensure that both he and his dog (whilst keeping to the correct position) are as close into the side of the highway as they can get. When a vehicle is heard, the handler should give the command "Stop" to the dog. Without a moment's hesitation, he drops the handle on the animal's back but retains the lead to go in front of the dog and - using the white stick as a probe in case there is a ditch into which he might tumble, or a tree into which he might crash - steps onto the grass verge, calling the dog after him. With practice, this manoeuvre can be quickly, smoothly and promptly effected. In fact, through repetition the dog itself will become familiar with this protective procedure, and will automatically stop, or at least slow-up, upon hearing a vehicle in proximity. Once the vehicle or vehicles have passed by, the handler steps back into the roadway, picks up the harness-handle, gives the command "Forward" and the unit resumes its journey. Of course, it will be much easier for a guide dog owner to go along a country road with which he is familiar, rather than an unknown one, since he will be better acquainted with the highway and its turnings and junctions, as well as with the terrain upon which he is walking when he takes evasive action to contend with approaching vehicles.

The blind person proceeding along a country road with a guide dog should walk on that side of the highway which is most convenient and comfortable for him. As well as the white harness of the dog making the unit more conspicuous to motorists, the handler should carry also a white stick in the free hand. During the hours of darkness it is especially unwise to go on country walks, but if necessity deems it the blind pedestrian's clothing should be of a light colour, and a reflective arm band should be worn, if not a fluorescent outer waistcoat similar to those used by many joggers and cyclists. Additionally useful is reflective material on the white stick, the dog's harness, and other parts of the person's clothing.

Variable climatic conditions

Night time walks with guide dogs should be undertaken at intermittent intervals. Dogs which work well in the day may not necessarily show the same propensity in the dark. Practice, therefore, under such conditions is a pre-requisite so that some measure of adequate performance exhibits itself in the moonlight as well as the sunlight. Also, by occasionally working the dog in the dark, imperfections of eyesight may come to light. For instance, there is a visual disease found in occasional dogs known as progressive retinal atrophy, colloquially known as 'night blindness'. Although prior veterinary examination will have diagnosed the complaint, later development of the condition, or only an imperceptible presence at the time of inspection, can mean that the disease is overlooked. However, as the name 'night blindness' suggests, afflicted canine eyesight becomes so imperfect whilst working in the dark, that its existence will very soon come to the notice of the handler by way of obstacle collision, poor right shoulder and crowd work, overshot kerbs and a general lack of effectiveness in the dog's performance.

Adverse weather conditions should not deter the trainer from venturing forth to work with his dogs. Fog, rain, snow, hail and storms may all need to be contended with at some time or another by the guide dog user, and if the animal has not previously been made thoroughly conversant with such weather conditions, it may baulk at going out in them, or at the least prove a most unwilling worker when so beset. Whilst some sympathy can be felt for the trainer who must perforce face all sorts of climatic conditions, for the sake of thorough training and habituation it is a necessary evil to put up with.

Wind, it is said, is the blind man's fog. Hearing is affected to the extent where sound localisation is made difficult because of gusting gales. It is thus difficult to 'read' the traffic situation on roads that need to be crossed, since the proximity and situation of moving vehicles is made difficult to assess as the sounds they make are tossed about in the wind. Extra care is therefore called for in these conditions. And when ice is on the ground, it is not a bad idea for the guide dog user to clip slip-proof attachments to his footwear.

Blindfold exercise

Little is to be gained from the practice, where it is exercised, of the trainer in blindfold walking his dog, usually over a known route, at that time when training is almost completed. Perhaps the student to whom the dog is shortly to be allocated will have his confidence boosted somewhat in the knowledge that the trainer is trusting enough to walk the animal while he is blindfolded, but the practice proves no great point beyond this, particularly if the idea is to determine any negative factors which may be present in the canine, and which now suddenly evidence themselves. The discerning trainer will have already noted such factors during preceding training, and not await an isolated exercise to discover them, when it is much too late to do anything about rectifying matters.

An additional reservation about the practice is that the dog, with previously a fluent handler following, now finds the same person producing an inept performance, notwithstanding the fact that walks in blindfold are invariably supervised by a training colleague in close attendance, to ensure that accidents do not ensue. Thus, the walk, although of comparatively short duration, can be a little upsetting to the canine.

Perhaps the exercise enlightens the trainer somewhat to the difficulties faced by a blind person when following a guide dog? It might also be useful for publicity purposes and exhibitions in front of admiring crowds of sighted spectators. One walk and a blindfold promptly removed, however, cannot allow an appreciation of the acute problems presented by blindness. The practice nevertheless does little harm, but on the other hand is hardly of worth either.

PART TWO: HOMO SAPIENS

"For man is man and master of his fate."
Alfred, Lord Tennyson (1809-1892)

—————— *10* ——————

ELIGIBILITY FOR TRAINING

To be eligible for training with a guide dog, an applicant must be registered blind. But this does not imply he is completely bereft of sight. Many guide dog owners have some useful residual vision. Of the registered blind population, only a small minority can be accepted for training. This is because the restrictions of old age (or under age - applicants must be over 18) or other disabilities, whether of a physical or mental nature, mitigate against owning a guide dog.

The current blind register of Great Britain, with a six figure total of entries, cannot be compared to many of the earlier returns and statistics, if only because less than 15 per cent of today's figures fall in the categories of total or sub-total blindness. In a population of 36,070,492 in the 1911 census, 26,336 people were registered blind; against this, and the 25,840 blind persons of 1919, the present-day blind register should consist (taking into account stricter guide lines of past years and modern improved ophthalmological surgery) of about 15,000 names. In other words, the blind of today are mostly sighted by the standards of another age. This leads to some confusion, because to the man in the street the term blind still carries the older connotation. Also, most of the blind in bygone days were young or middle-aged, whereas in England and Wales in 1977, 81,078 of the 110,040 on the register were over the age of 65. Trends are similar in Scotland, since at 31st December 1974, of the 10,063 blind, 6,812 were over the age of 65.

With present figures in Britain approaching 170,000 registered blind, the upsurge of elderly registrations continues unabated. Threequarters of the total on the register are over the age of 65; two-thirds are over the age of 80. In the United Kingdom there are about 200 blind people in every 100,000 of the general population. However, of those over 65 years the prevalence is 2,500. Above age 75 in Britain, the blindness incidence rate jumps to 7,000 in every 100,000 of the population in that age group. The way in which the blind register continues to dramatically increase can be seen when the 1976 total of 101,056 in England alone is compared to the 1986 figure of 120,548.

When we ask why blindness is related to old age, the answer lies in medical progress which keeps people living longer, whilst degenerative diseases continue. Medicine has not kept pace with increased life expectancy. And visual impairment with advancing years is one example.

It must be mentioned also that a significant number of visually handicapped people - beyond that formidable total registered as blind - are registered as partially sighted. Co-incidentally, the majority of partially sighted people are again elderly. In England in 1977 there were 45,400 persons registered as partially sighted, of whom 30,700 were over the age of 65. But, registration figures included, there are an estimated 250,000 persons in Britain with seriously defective vision, of whom 5,000 are totally blind. Additionally, there are many thousands of visually impaired people who do not need to use a white stick but who experience severe problems related to sight during their daily life.

Why do these figures conflict with the official statistics? It would be as well at this point to examine the procedures of registration and the definition of blindness. Only an ophthalmologist can register a person as blind or partially sighted, and such admission to the register is purely voluntary. When the patient is told by the ophthalmologist that he is of such poor vision that he could be included on the partially sighted or blind register, the person may refuse admission. If, therefore, the patient expresses the wish to be included on the register, he tacitly seeks the intervention of various voluntary agencies for the visually handicapped and of the statutory bodies. Other people, however, opt out, or do not consult an eye specialist in the first place, thus accounting for the increased estimate of visually impaired persons.

The three most common causes of blindness in Britain (and elsewhere in the Western world) are macular degeneration, cataract and glaucoma. These eye diseases are accountable for the visual loss of threequarters of the blind population, most commonly among the elderly.

The eye specialist tests his patient's sight using the Snellen's wall chart. The square-shaped serif letters on the test-types decrease in size as they go downwards on the chart. The letters are of such a size that the normal eye should discern the top one at 60 metres, while the following rows should be read at 36, 24, 18, 12, 9, 6 and 5 metres respectively. Being impracticable to see the type at these distances, it is usually placed six metres in front of the patient. The visual acuity is expressed as a fraction, the numerator signifying the distance of the patient from the chart, i.e. six metres, and the denominator indicating the distance at which the lowest or smallest row of letters is read by the unassisted eye.

A patient with normal vision should, six metres away from the chart, read the row of smallest letters and thus have his vision recorded as 6/6. On the other hand if a patient only perceives the fourth line on the chart, the visual acuity of this eye under test is 6/18. Should the patient be unable to read the bold, top letter, he is asked to approach nearer the chart. If he recognises the top letter at 3 metres, the visual acuity is 3/60. If he cannot read the top letter no matter how close, he is asked to count fingers held against a dark background: perception of the fingers at 3 metres is recorded as counts fingers (C.F.) at 3m. Sometimes, where visual acuity is even further affected, the patient may only recognise hand movements at 2 metres, which is noted as H.M. at 2m. With an even greater reduction of vision, light is shone on the eye and it is ascertained if there is perception of light, recorded on the BD8 as P.L.

Ideally, the test-type, which is black on white, should be evenly illuminated, the chart should be about the level of the patient's eyes and he should have his back to any windows. The vision of each eye is tested separately as well as together. N.P.L. on the BD8 denotes no perception of light. The patient is literally one of that very small minority who is totally blind.

When the ophthalmologist finds that a patient has a visual capability of 3/60 or less, then this person is eligible for blind registration. Where the sight is above 3/60 but below 6/60 then this indicates registration as a partially sighted person. However, for the purposes of registration, field of vision is also taken into account. Thus, a person with 6/60 visual acuity (or even above) but having a contracted field of vision might well be eligible for blind registration. As two examples, a person with retinitis pigmentosa (tunnel vision) may well be registered as blind because of his limited field of vision, and yet be able to read a book. Similarly, a person with macular degeneration (where the central vision is affected) and consequently registered blind, might find himself capable of watching, in reasonable comfort, the television. It must be pointed out that the eye tests and results are carried out with uncorrected vision, so that where a person - without spectacles - has a visual capability of less than 3/60, he would not be registered blind if, wearing glasses, his vision was above 6/60; also, of course, if there were no field of vision loss.

The ophthalmologist will need to be reasonably tactful when discussing failing vision with a patient. On being told that his loss of vision is sufficient for registration, a patient may be quite overwhelmed and wrongly assume that because he is now called 'blind' he will eventually lose his sight altogether.

The form BD8, the certificate of registration, which is completed by the ophthalmologist, is sent to the Social Work Department serving the area in which the newly-registered patient lives, and the referral is allocated to the Social Worker for the Visually impaired. The ever increasing numbers of blind people (as noted before, specifically the elderly blind) places - in keeping with social work trends generally - some measure of strain upon the resources of the statutory bodies.

It has been mentioned that the three main causes of blindness are Macular Degeneration, Cataracts and Glaucoma. Briefly, Macular Degeneration (as the name implies) is a degenerative complaint affecting the macula (central) portion of the eye. The peripheral vision remains relatively unaffected, although as time goes on the blotted-out part of the eye becomes greater. The vision may be satisfactory for some years, but steadily decreases, although not totally. The visual defect affects only the central vision, and binocular spectacles or a magnifying glass can help overcome the difficulty so that the remaining sight is made full use of.

Cataracts (we refer here to senile Cataract) are rarely seen before the age of 40, but become more frequent in succeeding decades. Cataracts are observed as mist-like opacities which affect the lens of the eye, and whose opacity becomes more intense with increasing age. Where other eye conditions are not present, cataracts are operable and sight, using corrective glasses, can be quite markedly restored.

Glaucoma is a building-up of internal pressure in the globe of the eye. This raised intraocular pressure not only affects vision adversely, but causes much discomfort to the sufferer. When detected in the early stages, however, Glaucoma may be stabilised with treatment. Although improvement is not effected, sight no longer deteriorates.

From the fore-going it will be noted that blindness is therefore not equated with total loss of vision; in fact, only five per cent of the blind population are completely without sight.

A survey by the local university of the visually handicapped residents of Nottingham (336 blind and 205 partially sighted people) revealed that rather than having been totally blind from birth, and having blindness as their only disability, they tended to be elderly, to have become visually handicapped later in life, to have some residual vision, and to have an additional impairment. More than two-thirds of the subjects in the survey were over retirement age, and less than 14 per cent of them were born with their visual handicap. Over 70 per cent of them could see more than just light perception, and well over half of the total of those interviewed had another illness or disability in addition to their visual problem.

The registered blind population is preponderantly elderly; among new registrations those aged 90 and over contribute almost as many as all age groups up to and including 50 years of age. In the United States also the majority of blind persons are old. It is clear that the needs of elderly blind people represent a growing problem. Almost by definition the aged blind are multiply handicapped, and many have additional ailments. And the difficulties that beset all elderly persons are compounded with the addition of visual impairment, such as transportation and mobility problems, social isolation and inadequate nutrition. Although late onset blindness is not usually total, the loss of the ability to read and write, to see a television screen clearly, and to get around unaided are severe handicaps for those no longer young.

With blindness being a handicap which affects mainly the elderly, and since most of this sector of the population will be unable to use guide dogs, should this form of mobility therefore warrant the attention it attracts, and expenditure it involves? The answer is in the affirmative, because for the younger blind person, and active not-so-young, the guide dog is an admirable mobility tool, a good companion, a deterrent to night-time intruders, and a focus for social interchange. It can be argued that elderly people, even with unaffected vision, are limited in their mobility and independence anyway, but for a younger person to be restricted in this way is disastrous. A guide dog affords some measure of freedom to those who might otherwise be considerably confined both in movement and access.

The diseases of the eye affecting the younger individual include Glaucoma, but Cataracts and Macular Degeneration are less-often met up with amongst students for guide dog training. More commonly will be seen persons blinded through accident, but additionally will be those students who suffer from the lesser known but nevertheless comparatively prevalent eye complaints, some of which might be linked to other physical symptoms.

Diabetes is a case in point. Diabetic retinopathy is more likely to enforce early retirement than any other eye condition in the advanced countries of the world. One in six of every blind individual under the age of 65 is diabetic. Diabetes ensues when the body fails to metabolise carbohydrates because of insulin deficiency, or of a proliferation of another hormone, glucagon. Insulin and glucagon are stored and secreted by the pancreas. Because the diabetic is an individual whose body fails to deal with sugars and starches as it should in order to ensure maximum efficiency and well-being, it is necessary to offset this by appropriate medical measures. Thus, the treatment of diabetes consists of the administration of insulin either orally or by injection. Additional drugs may also be prescribed in order to control the level of blood sugar.

117

Diabetes is a complex condition which can affect a number of systems in the body. The sense of touch is lessened, for instance, and consequent reaction to pain. Extremities of the body are particularly affected, and are therefore prone to damage. And since the healing processes to bruised and lacerated tissues tend to take longer, the diabetic needs to expend extra care to avoid injury.

A more serious aspect of diabetes - but which does not affect all sufferers - is a consequence of the retinopathy which results when haemorrhages are caused through rupture of the tiny blood vessels which feed the retina at the back of the eye; a consequence which can conclude with visual impairment.

The spillage of blood from the broken vessels prevents light, in part, from reaching the retina, thus causing loss of sight to a greater or lesser extent. Often, however, these haemorrhages are minor and are spontaneously absorbed, so that loss of vision may be only for a brief period and useful sight is restored. Unfortunately, the trouble is prone to recur at periodic intervals. With the passage of time, and formation of scar tissue from repeated haemorrhages, sight is liable to be permanently affected. An additional complication is the possibility of detached retina through contraction of scar tissue pulling that vital rear window of the eye out of place.

Physical exertion, resulting in an increased blood supply, particularly to the head, should be avoided by the diabetic. Not to the exclusion of all exercise, however, since walking and swimming, for instance, are to be encouraged. What is to be avoided, though, are such things as moving heavy furniture or other weights, bending down and scrubbing floors, pushing cars that won't start, and similar strenuous activities.

All individuals suffering from diabetic retinopathy do not become blind, and the course of the complaint is such that vision may fluctuate, so that the person will find that he can see better on some days than others. Diabetes is unfortunately such that, as well as an ultimate tendency to possible detached retinas, the eye is also more susceptible to cataract and glaucoma.

It is important that the guide dog trainer be acquainted with the disease diabetes since, where he is teaching a student suffering from diabetic retinopathy, it may be that the instructor will meet up with one of the reactions brought about by the complaint and which affects the trainee.

The intake of insulin, and a carefully planned diet, coupled with the amount of exercise undertaken, needs to be precisely balanced by the diabetic so that no side effects ensue. Where adverse reactions do occur, however, it is important that the guide dog trainer both recognises them accurately, and treats them accordingly.

The two most likely complications to be encountered by the diabetic are coma and insulin reaction. If too much insulin (over-treated diabetes) is absorbed by the body, or if food intake is lessened, altered or delayed, or - and this is important to the guide dog trainer - physical activity is increased too dramatically, all of these can lead to a lowering of the sugar level in the blood.

As the body reacts to a low sugar level (hypoglycaemia), which is a condition where there is a deficiency of glucose in the blood, the sufferer becomes pale, weak, hungry, shivers and sweats profusely and respiration is rapid and shallow. Body movements are unco-ordinated, and speech and thought unclear. If left untreated, insulin reaction results in unconsciousness.

Most diabetics carry with them on their person some form of sugar - a sugar lump, sweet soft drink or a concentrated glucose mint. The treatment for insulin reaction is the immediate administration of sugar in one form or another, and since most diabetics can recognise the onset of hypoglycaemia, they are swift to suck a sugar lump or glucose mint, or swallow a sweet soft drink. The wise guide dog trainer, when instructing a blind diabetic, will similarly carry such sweet stuffs with him, should his student suffer a hypoglycaemia attack and has forgotten his own sugar or glucose lumps.

Because of the increased activity involved in guide dog training, the diabetic might consequently be more prone to insulin reaction. Where the sufferer lapses into unconsciousness - although appropriate measures as outlined will prevent this from taking place - medical help should be summoned for the purposes of a glucagon injection.

Diabetes coma (under-treated diabetes) is a less-frequent condition than insulin reaction, and onset is slower. Because under-treated diabetes cannot burn up the carbohydrates in the system, the body resorts to the use of fats as a source of energy, through which sugar in the blood reaches excess levels. This in turn brings about an over-concentration of poisonous fatty acids circulating throughout the system, a condition known as ketosis which can result in diabetic coma, or hyperglycaemia.

Preceding coma, and acting as warning lights to both the diabetic and to the guide dog trainer, are the symptoms of hyperglycaemia, viz., nausea, lethargy, thirst, dry skin and laboured breathing. To remedy this serious situation, insulin dosage, and water and salt intake, are vital.

Hypoglycaemia and hyperglycaemia must be diligently differentiated. The consequence of wrong dosage administration, if symptoms of the two conditions are confused, are serious. The aftermath of giving glucose, instead of insulin, to a person in a hyperglycaemia coma, and insulin, instead of glucose, to a diabetic in a hypoglycaemic coma, could be disastrous.

When instructing the blind diabetic, the guide dog trainer should bear in mind that strict adherence to the agency time-table may not fit in with the physical needs to this particular student. A planned activity may have to be adjusted where it co-incides with a meal time or rest period which is essential to the student. Even so, the trainer will need to be on the alert for signs of a diabetic coma or insulin reaction since, for those students who are not used to strenuous exercise, increased activity may result in a drop of blood sugar level. Insulin dosage adjustment may need to be made. Training periods immediately after a meal, when low blood sugar is less likely to be contended with, are best for diabetics. A gradual increase in physical exertion as the training course goes on, rather than a full programme from day one, is also a wise precaution when teaching the diabetic student.

As well as the additional physical diabetic complications which may present themselves during guide dog training, such as indifferent balance and possible lack of co-ordination, and leg and foot health problems caused by poor circulation due to failing blood vessels, the instructor should be aware of the emotional and psychological imbalances that his student might display.

Fluctuating blood sugar levels inevitably temporarily affect the personality of the individual. When blood sugar is low, the diabetic may be antagonistic, moody, nervous, or excited. If blood sugar is high, the person may be happy or manic, and with diabetic coma looming, the student will be lethargic and drowsy. The state of the mind can affect the body, and when a diabetic is upset or angry, the disease may be harder to control. The guide dog trainer should therefore not unnecessarily create conflict with his student, no matter how justified the instructor may feel sharp criticism is warranted.

The diabetic is prone to infection, even gangrene, from comparatively minor cuts and bruises. Without indulging his student, since, notwithstanding the disease, a relatively normal life can still be led, the guide dog trainer should thus be on his guard to prevent accidents (for instance, kicking and stumbling over an up-kerb, or colliding with a post) which might, to a non-diabetic, be considered minor. All guide dogs are good, but those allocated to blind diabetics must be especially so.

Diabetes has been dwelt upon at length in this chapter because it is the major single cause of blindness among those of working age in this country, and consequently, with the guide dog being a favourite form of safe mobility for so many sufferers, the diabetic student will be frequently encountered by the guide dog trainer. It is important that he is aware of the implications in training a blind diabetic with a guide dog. At the same time, with the help of the training staff, the diabetic should endeavour to keep strictly to his medical routine and diet at all times, and be aware of vacillating blood sugar levels which might possibly arise during guide dog training. He should also be aware of advances in ophthalmological science which may help to preserve his eyesight. If diabetes sufferers have had the disease for more than 10 years, this unfortunately increases the chance of damage to the eyes. With regular screening signs of deteriorating vision might be detected in the early stages, and laser treatment of diabetic retinopathy may prevent the visual condition from progressing.

Although the overwhelming majority of visually handicapped people are elderly, it nevertheless remains that each year some 2,000 individuals between the ages of 16 and 65 are registered as blind. We have seen that about 12 per cent of blind registrations approximating to this age range suffer from diabetic retinopathy. A few will be registered, notwithstanding comparative youth, because of macular degeneration and cataracts, but, after diabetes, the bigger percentage will be victim to glaucoma. Besides congenital and adventitious causes of blindness, retinal detachment, which might occur in varying degrees due to a tear or a hole in the retina thus occluding light reception at the back of the eye, is responsible for many registrations in the younger age groups. When a retina is totally detached, blindness in that eye ensues. In some cases surgery can be effective in repairing a partially, or even completely detached retina.

Where surgical intervention is of no avail at all, however, is in the instance of optic atrophy, which is due to the wasting away of the nerve fibres connecting the eye to the brain, resulting in interrupted, and perhaps total lack of vision.

Albinism is often a cause of weak visual perception; this hereditary complaint, marked by lack of pigment in the hair and skin, and iris of the eye, is sometimes accompanied by other sight disorders severe enough to warrant blind registration. Responsible, too, for a growing number of registrations in the younger age range is another hereditary condition known as retinitis pigmentosa, which, as the name suggests, is also associated with misplaced pigment, but this time affecting only the eye (although there is often an accompanying hearing defect) and leading to degeneration and, sometimes, total atrophy of the retina. Less explicable as a cause of visual loss is amblyopia, which can only be described as poor sight without any apparent identifiable disease of the eye. The condition is such, however, that the sufferer is more often registered as partially sighted as opposed to being considered blind.

*   *   *   *

A blind person, according to the legal definition, "should be so blind as to be unable to perform any work for which eyesight is essential". Work in this context is not seen purely in terms of employment, but concerned with all those tasks that need to be undertaken during our day-to-day lives. It is nonetheless true that many people registered as blind will retain, in some instances, what appears to be a remarkable residue of vision, especially when one might naturally equate blindness with a total loss of sight.

It is those blind people with good residual vision who might present problems to the instructors involved in training them with guide dogs. Not so much in the areas of individual assimilation of knowledge, or application of practical skills, but more in connection with the morale of the class as a whole. Since this student with some sight, which he now uses to good effect whilst out walking with his dog, will seldom find difficulties in training, his fellow classmates will perhaps feel a little demoralized when comparing their standards and progress (although the trainer will have warned them previously of the futility of such antithesis) with his. From another point of view, the person with reasonable residual vision may rely so much on his remaining sight that he finds himself unable to build up confidence in his dog. This in turn affects the animal so that poor canine performance ensues, simply because the student is not demanding enough of, or stringent enough with, the dog (which is now becoming aware that the new handler does not expect high standards of compliance), since it is he, in fact, who is exerting the guiding influence over the unit, much though he tries to will himself not to, rather than the other way about.

The handler cannot be disparaged for assuming leadership in this way, disturbing though it is to the trainer. It is simply that the student finds himself unable to desist from using his residual vision. Other class-members, however, wonder why he never trips at up-kerbs, or encounters difficulties with canine anticipation at corners, or always negotiates obstacles superbly, and manages traffic well and never suffers from shoddy right shoulder work. On the other hand, in variable lighting conditions, such as differences between bright and overcast days, or night-time walks, problems might be presented which, to some extent, bewilder this usually capable student. Similarly, a handler with deteriorating sight, having trained with his dog when his vision was comparatively good, will possibly face hardship in managing his mobility with the passage of time because of poor control and following and lack of confidence in his dog.

Experiments in blindfolding the student who retains residual vision whilst undergoing training with a guide dog are rather futile exercises. One cannot expect a person, previously with some vision, to immediately adapt to total blindness when such a traumatic event would normally take many months, if not years, of adjustment. And now he is expected to become mobile with, and take control of, a guide dog. Even if this student struggled through the training course completely blacked out, it is doubtful if he would persist in continuing as 'totally blind' for mobility purposes during the ensuing years at home. Furthermore, for whatever endeavours, blind people with residual vision are constantly encouraged to use their remaining sight to its best advantage.

The blind person with some sight thus poses problems both for himself and the trainer concerned, not to mention the canine, when he undertakes mobility training with a guide dog. Nevertheless, since he is registered as blind, and so is perfectly eligible for training, and, complexities mitigating against a successful partnership with his dog notwithstanding, for all the problems posed the team often develops into a reasonably worthwhile unit through a continuing process of adaptation on both sides. If the blind person's eye condition is stable, and even though he himself is the main implement of mobility, the dog can at least make up for any slight deficiencies in human pedestrian travel as well as providing some impetus for the owner to get out and about. And if the guide dog owner's sight is gradually diminishing, then over the months the quality of work displayed might not be of a high calibre since the dog, with the passage of time, now has to assume the mantle (which under normal circumstances it would have originally worn) of safe mobility manager - previously the precinct of the handler - at least the two might make reasonably sound travel progress, effected through continuing adjustment and modification on both sides. The only substance lacking, and this of a crucial nature, might be the extreme confidence in his dog which all blind handlers should exhibit.

To perform well as a guide, the dog must inwardly feel, as far as that is possible for an unreasoning yet perceptive animal, the confidence and rapport which should be exuded by the handler. If the owner is hesitant and uncertain, the dog will be similarly so. Without the intrepidity and authority of the handler, and without the sparkling clarity and encouragement of positive verbal entreaties to back this boldness up, the dog itself will lack punch and directiveness. It will be hesitant at kerbs, unsure at obstacles, indecisive in traffic, lax at right shoulder work, and weak in willingness. All of these canine inadequacies can only be countered by honest human resolve and assertiveness.

11

INTERVIEWING THE APPLICANT

To determine a person's potential and suitability for guide dog training, his probable trainer (but failing that a colleague who will report back) should conduct an interview in the applicant's home area. In this way the blind person's geographical knowledge of his own locale, together with awareness of environmental features, can best be measured. Not only will this information be gleaned during general conversation, but the applicant, escorted by the trainer, will go out for a walk of some length in the home surrounds. During the walk, the trainer will guide the blind person as would a dog, thus giving the applicant an inkling of what it feels like to work with a guide dog. Additionally, the trainer will, during his observations of the applicant whilst they are out walking together, gather some useful technical information that will help him decide which of his dogs would best suit this particular person.

Holding the open end of the U-shaped harness-handle in his right hand, the trainer shows the blind person how to grasp the handhold on the opposite extremity. This is loosely held in the upturned fingers of the left hand, with the arm straight down at the side, and barely bent at the elbow. The palm of the hand faces to the rear.

To assess verbal capacity for canine control, as well as modulation, which matters so much when working with a dog, the trainer will ask the applicant to give the command "Forward" and other directional injunctions during this evaluation exercise. The applicant will also be requested to employ both negative and positive verbal reinforcement, for the benefit of the interviewing trainer, and, to test practical potential, after having first been given a demonstration, the blind person will display his prowess at physically correcting a dog.

By so doing, the trainer will note from the applicant's abilities with regard to this whether a 'hard' or a 'soft' dog would best suit the blind person. The instructor will be additionally swayed in this direction by the applicant's hold on the harness-handle: is it severe or is it gentle, and does he follow diligently or clumsily as he walks along escorted by the trainer (acting the part of the dog) on his left? Is he soft footed or heavy footed; does he walk quickly or slowly; does he have any peculiarities of gait? These factors also will have a bearing on the category of dog to be assigned to the applicant.

During the walk the blind person is asked: in which street are we now? What is the name of the shop (or school, or factory, or office) we are near? Where is the nearest telephone or post box? Could you take me (the trainer) back to your home from this point? In this way the applicant's awareness of his home surroundings can be measured; such local knowledge will be most useful in guide dog ownership by getting the partnership off to a confident start through firm directional indication to an uninitiated - as far as this area is concerned - animal by the handler. A deep familiarity with the home environs also indicates intelligence, interest and perception on the part of the person insofar as enhancing his own orientation and mobility is concerned. Allowance must naturally be made for someone who has recently moved into a new area, and it must also be stressed that, though knowledge of one's local environment is of considerable help in guide dog work, nevertheless a lack of this knowledge would not preclude an applicant from the training course. And where awareness of the locale needs to be heightened, in the interim period whilst awaiting guide dog training – and indeed thereafter - familiarity with the home environment can be gradually improved.

The trainer will observe the applicant's posture. Does he stand erect and look forward in a composed manner, as is normal, or does he lean to one side, or bend backwards in the hope of protecting his face that little more in case of collision? Indeed, it will be such nasty encounters in the past that have brought about this tendency, which is thus seen to be a natural, although, for a future guide dog owner, an undesirable consequence. These postural deficiencies will need to be taken into account when matching this person with a guide dog.

How safe is the applicant regarding traffic? Does he have a good road sense? It is the guide dog owner, after all, who accepts responsibility for the safety of the unit. The trainer will test the blind person's traffic awareness by, at a suitable down-kerb where moving vehicles are apparent, asking him to give the command "Forward" at an opportune and safe moment. This exercise will be repeated to doubly ascertain the safety factor. Where this factor is lacking, the blind person will need to vastly improve his road sense before consideration is given to his application for a guide dog. Only through practice and utmost caution will traffic safety skills from the pedestrian point of view be enhanced. With the application of common sense, it is by no means beyond the powers of the average blind person who is not as safety conscious as he should be

126

to correct this fault. The trainer will advise the applicant, whilst he is waiting for training with a guide dog, to build up his expertise in dealing safely with busy road junctions. This will extend to seeking sighted help in instances where the blind person finds it impossible to embark on a road crossing alone.

What of the applicant's reflexes? Are they quick or slow? Bearing in mind the speed of his reactions, could he promptly and successfully correct a dog if it made a mistake? The trainer will test sensibility by, for instance, over-shooting a shallow down-kerb with the applicant following, and without forewarning him. Is the applicant quick to stop and query the situation? And when the trainer deliberately brushes the person he is guiding into an over-hanging privet hedge, does the person promptly take avoiding action? These reactions will be taken into account when final assessment is made regarding acceptability for training and when matching dog with person.

A most important attribute for a guide dog applicant is motivation. If this is high, it can often outweigh any negative features. To be considered additionally is the applicant's place of work (if employed) and routes commonly used with note taken of the differing conditions to contend with on these journeys. A person dwelling in a big, busy city bears different requirements by way of a guide dog than does someone who lives and works in the heart of the country and seldom, if ever, ventures into town.

At interview, it is important that the negative aspects (if such they could be called) of guide dog ownership are discussed between trainer and applicant. Is the family happy to have a dog in the home? If not, who voices objections, and why? Can the trainer allay any doubts on the part of such an objector? Often, a few words of explanation from the trainer can alleviate any fears which might be felt by a family member regarding a large dog coming into the home. This person, for instance, may be under the misapprehension that a guide dog is aggressive and protective; or that, since it is a bitch, at certain times of the year it will attract the amorous attentions of the neighbourhood's wandering canine Casanovas.

Nevertheless, facts must be faced regarding the responsibilities of dog ownership. For example, in wet and snowy conditions, a damp dog can be a bit of a liability in a spotless house. However, a good towelling before admittance will help solve this problem. Muddy paws on carpets might also not be welcomed by the lady of the house. These offending paws, too, will need to be dried out. And if the dog is ill-behaved (which it should not if the guide dog owner is, as instructed, firm with his charge) in the presence of other people, there are those visitors who would not particularly relish muddy canine paw marks or scratches on new clothes, caused by an unruly over-friendly animal jumping up at them.

One must bear in mind the inconvenience suffered by the owner, and indeed family, if the dog falls ill. Vomit on a new carpet, perhaps, coupled with the other consequences of an upset stomach or infected bladder. Not to mention the heart-ache caused the family by such canine illness, and, in old age, debility, and finally, parting.

Finance must be considered, feeding and veterinary expenditure not least, although some agencies offer assistance to defray these costs. And, on cold, wet, windy winter days and nights, the animal must still have the obligatory exercise to obey the calls of nature, no matter the hour. And in the summer, when the dog casts its winter coat, the all-pervading and multitudinous animal hairs will no doubt arouse the displeasure of the housekeeper.

A formidable number of negative points, then, for the would-be guide dog owner, and his family, to consider before entering into a partnership with a canine escort. But at the same time the trainer will enumerate the positive points which, overall, at least for most people, will well out-weigh the negative features.

There can be little doubt, it is worth expounding, that after a demanding, testing, stressful and at times uncomfortable and painful three or four weeks of initial guide dog instruction, the new owner will return home a person better equipped to cope with his handicap, be more resourceful and physically and mentally competent, and, most of all, as far as his mobility aid is concerned, be an able and confident dog handler. And as the first few faltering months at home pass by, the reward to be reaped will be that of safe and independent pedestrian travel through a trusting and equable partnership with a responsive guide dog. Because of this refreshing resurgence of spirit and adventure in the previously less-mobile blind person, his family too will welcome into the household their four-footed addition, and will delight also in the companionship and fun this simple dog has brought with it.

On a more sombre note, in those isolated and unhappy instances where a blind person's application for guide dog training is turned down, and he feels himself to be unfairly judged, he should retain the right to be interviewed by another trainer or official from the agency concerned to confirm or deny the earlier decision. If confirmed, and the applicant is still dissatisfied, he can of course apply to another agency (if such an alternative is available) in the hope that perhaps he will be accepted for training by this second organisation. Invariably, however, trainers the world over broadly agree on both human and canine standards of acceptability within which a successful outcome to training can be countenanced.

The dog is prepared to stop in the eventuality of the car ahead reversing across the unit's path into the road from the garage forecourt.

A newly-qualified guide dog user poses happily with her bright-eyed black Labrador.

A parked car on a road without sidewalks proves to be an obstacle which the guide dog unit negotiates unerrimgly on this occasion. The trainer observes in the background.

The sylvan setting of the Exeter training centre provides an ideal backdrop for this group of qualifying guide dog users.

The blind person and guide dog are preparing to cross the road, but before so doing are aware of the oncoming traffic, and must allow this to clear before leaving the down-kerb. Note that the dog has been trained to work on the right of this particular gentleman because of his permanently weak and deformed left arm.

The correct position at the down-kerb prior to crossing the road, with both man and dog facing straight ahead.

A trainer in blindfold tries out his dog.

The correct grip and arm position is being described to the applicant by the guide dog trainer.

The dog is not only awaiting the passage of the train, but also the uplifting of the barriers. Although the dog could easily proceed under the barrier, the handler would come into collision with it; the animal is therefore trained to allow for the height and width of the accompanying person.

Mother and father watch as their son sets off with his guide dog under the scrutiny of the trainer, who is on an after-care visit.

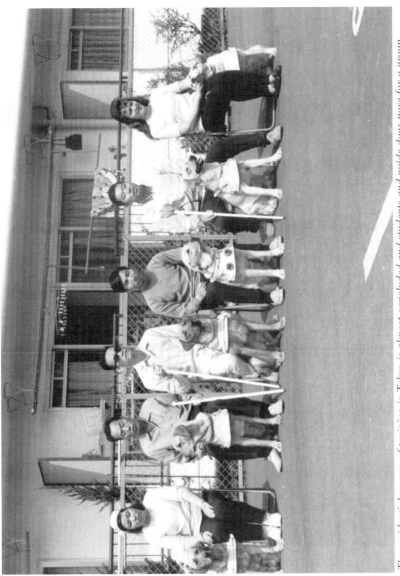

The residential course of training in Tokyo is almost concluded and students and guide dogs pose for a group photograph.

Although the grid on the sidewalk has made the dog a little apprehensive about its own safety as far as its paws are concerned, nevertheless it has successfully completed a good kerb approach, ensuring the protection of the handler from collision with the nearby post, and now awaits the command to move off.

A happy guide dog user with a fine yellow Labrador of good concentration prepares to cross the road. The unit occupies an ideal stance at the down-kerb.

Waiting for the lights to change. The guide dog owner listens carefully. It is he who must decide when it is safe to cross.

An artificial obstacle training session.

Where possible, use of pedestrian bridges across busy roads is advisable.

12

MATCHING

The matching of a guide dog to a blind person has seemingly become more involved with the passing years since those days when Dorothy Harrison Eustis first established her guide dog training facility in Switzerland. Her comments at that time regarding the pairing of blind person and guide dog were brief: "Next comes the question of placing the right dog with the right man, for different temperaments and characters need different handling and those of man and dog must complement each other".

As the guide dog movement spread further afield, and as training methods became more intense and dog selection more refined and guide dog schools more sophisticated, so that crucial and initial match of dog and man appears to have grown in magnitude and complexity. Leading up to the pairing of the two so that a workmanlike unit will result once team training is successfully completed, is the total assessment of the blind person by his trainer (precipitated by previous interview in the applicant's home area, which many guide dog schools undertake) before allocation of the dog.

Of course, not every blind person can be matched with a guide dog. At interview it might be concluded that a blind person (usually for reasons of a personal physical or mental nature) is not of the right quality for a dog, and therefore it would be impossible to match him with any canine, let alone one optimally suited to his individual characteristics and environment. In other words, in the opinion of the guide dog school, the failed applicant could not be matched with a suitable dog no matter the excellence of such a dog.

In the United Kingdom, of the 492 blind persons who applied for guide dogs to the largest British agency, the Guide Dogs for the Blind Association, in an average year,

49 of these applicants were turned down. That is, 10 percent of would-be guide dog users. During the same period, two percent of accepted applicants failed to graduate, so that it will be noted that, even where blind persons attend for training, a minute minority fail to make the grade.

One of the reasons put forward to account for such failure may be that of a mis-match. However, it is seldom that such an event occurs. Of the overwhelming majority of guide dog units who graduate, do we account for the high success rate by pointing to the professional expertise and perception of the individual trainer concerned when the initial match of man and dog was made, or do we conjecture that, adhering to an assortment of very broad guide lines when teaming the two together, a happy outcome would result anyway?

Visiting a training centre the author Tim Heald felt that, having assessed their pupils, the trainers decide "on an allocation of dogs on a simple and obvious rule of thumb: tall dogs for tall people, boisterous ones for confident, placid for the nervous, quiet and steady for the old, dominant for the young". Perhaps this is an over-simplification of the matching process, which after all is quite searching and comprehensive, and upon which rests the difference between both human and canine success or failure.

Assigning a dog to a student begins well before the blind person attends the school for training. It starts from the moment he returns his application form to the training centre, together with the obligatory medical report from his family doctor. With the information gleaned from these two documents, the trainer will already have an inkling of the type of dog which would be appropriate to this particular person, not to mention whether or not he would be suitable for training in the first place. Taken into consideration, and accountable for in the application and medical forms, will be data such as personal health, degree and cause of visual loss, age, additional handicaps, height and weight, environmental conditions both at home and place of employment, and family circumstances.

Obviously, an applicant with a young family will require a dog which will be at ease amongst children. A worker at the factory bench all day will want an animal prepared to lie quietly under the work top for hours at a stretch, and which is not bothered by the noise and dirt of the manufacturing plant. A piano tuner would seek a dog with initiative above the average, which will remember particular clients' houses and ports of call, and which is willing to work a long and possibly wearing day.

A perusal of the interview report will help to indicate an appropriate assignation of guide dog to blind person. When considering a desirable match, the trainer will thus lay great store by the interview from the point of view of personal characteristics and ability. He will also take into account, but perforce to a considerably lesser extent, the wishes of the applicant as to a specific breed of dog which he might have requested.

At the commencement of the team training period, the first two days spent by the trainer with the student does not include any canine presence at all. Usually, it is on the third day that the dogs and students are introduced to each other. The initial couple of days are spent in assessing the student in order to corroborate or repudiate the wisdom of the pencilled-in match of man and dog which has already been formulated in the mind of the trainer, based on his own interview of the applicant, or that of a colleague, at some previous date.

Height and weight are checked so that an animal of suitable physique, sufficient to afford balance to the proposed unit, will be allocated. In this respect, distance of fingertips - with arm by the side - to ground level will be considered, since this too will have a bearing on the size of dog fitted for this particular candidate.

If a tall person is given a short dog, the guiding propensity suffers a little because of the decreased contact and 'togetherness' of the two, due to the necessity for a longer harness-handle, and also the more oblique angle at which this must now be held (see Figure 12-1). A good physical match between man and dog accords balance and a pleasing look to the unit, and the blind person feels more comfortable and assured whilst following such a well-suited animal as far as bodily proportions are concerned.

Figure 12-1

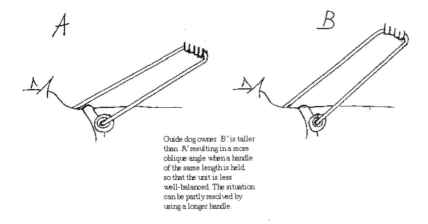

Guide dog owner B' is taller than A' resulting in a more oblique angle when a handle of the same length is held, so that the unit is less well-balanced. The situation can be partly resolved by using a longer handle.

131

This is not to say, however, that a fine match cannot take place between the tall person and the shorter dog. Sound temperament, speed of walking, willingness, initiative, adequate conditioning, socialisation and habituation play an even more important role in the matching of man and dog.

For the first couple of days training the instructor is going to play the part of the dog. By so doing he will be enabled to arrive at his final decision regarding the proposed match between man and canine. Leading the student around whilst he holds the harness-handle at the 'dog' end, with the student taking the opposite extremity in the prescribed manner, allows the trainer the opportunity to ascertain the blind person's physical capacity and verbal potential (in relation to control over his dog), degree of residual vision, if any, and to determine balance, gait, posture and speed of walking. In addition to this, the trainer can check on the student's response to untoward events (stepping unexpectedly over a kerb; brushing into a hedge), to further measure orientation skills and individual human characteristics, to assess ability regarding safety precautions, and any additional handicaps or peculiarities.

By observing and assessing each individual's interpretation and reactions to this simulation of the movements of the animal, the way it swerves as it deviates from a straight course if avoidance is needed as it walks along, and the manner of stopping and then starting off again, the trainer may, with some confidence - taking account of this and all previous relevant information - at last match a particular dog with a particular person. And yet, in the rare event of a mis-match, the trainer reserves the right, during ensuing training, to swap the first choice dog - where it is obvious events aren't working out as they should - with one of his two reserve animals. Here we see the wisdom of the trainer selecting, handling, and bringing up to class standard six dogs, notwithstanding the fact he will be dealing with only four students during team training.

In addition, the student is now more aware of the manner of following a guide dog, and the appropriate actions to take to suit particular circumstances, having practised such techniques on his trainer. He will now feel more confident in the handling of the animal when he is shortly allocated with it. Also, since the student has gained at least a modicum of proficiency in guide dog handling skills, the animal will not have to bear the brunt of total inexperience which might otherwise have an adverse effect on the introductory training walks when the two go out together as a team. In other words, the dog will not be as inhibited as it might be if the new handler had not acquired previous practical and verbal competence under the preliminary tuition of the trainer.

Perhaps it is superfluous to mention that matching must not be looked at in isolation, and it would be unethical to subsume the pairing as such. Matching is very much a matter of previous training, bearing in mind the assessment by the trainer of the blind applicant at initial interview. In this way, advance human data now having been correlated in the preceding weeks before class-training (training of blind student and guide dog together) the dog will be manipulated, as far as that is possible, to fit in with the environmental requirements, and capabilities and characteristics and psyche of the applicant. Thus it will be seen that matching a guide dog to student is often the culmination of (once the basic physical and mental makeup of the blind person has been ascertained) previous training and adaptation of the animal in such a way that it is going to be well suited to that specific blind person.

Whilst it is true that there is no such person as "Mr Average", or such an animal as "Average Dog", nevertheless, during training it is found that a number, indeed the majority of canines present themselves as - more or less - dogs with very much in common. Often enough also, guide dog applicants present similar physical and temperamental types. This is not to suggest that all of these dogs are *identical* to one another, or all of these people are *identical* to one another. One accepts all of them, human and canine, as individuals with individual likes and dislikes, individual physical and temperamental traits, and individual idiosyncrasies.

Of course, differences in the human are infinitely more acute as opposed to that simple creature, the dog. Also, the different environments in which people live must be taken into account when applications for guide dogs are being considered. Notwithstanding this, we are left with a large pool of dogs which enjoy a common grouping; similarly, albeit on a more sophisticated and complex level, we have also a large pool of guide dog applicants who might be considered as a common sector of humanity.

The contention being led to is that one of a number of guide dogs will be suitable for one of a number of people. This, therefore, makes the matching of dogs to people a good deal easier than might at first sight appear. In other words, Applicant "A" would be equally suited to Guide Dogs "A", "B", "C" or "D", whilst Guide Dog "A" might equally be suited to Applicants "A", "B", "C" or "D". Nevertheless, minor variations of character or environment might influence final allocation decisions. For instance, an applicant for a guide dog who lives in a rural area would be assigned with the animal (from "A", "B", "C" and "D") which shows least interest in farm animals, all other things being equal. Additionally, the perceptive trainer will have previously trained that particular dog earmarked for the rural dweller to walk discriminately along country roads and farm tracks.

It might now be claimed that, having satisfied the two provisos cited, then this animal (let us assume it is Guide Dog "A") is now the optimum dog for this particular country dweller, Applicant "A". However, what happens if Guide Dog "A", whilst free-running in the paddock, drops dead? The short answer is that the trainer now shuffles the pack and decides to allocate Applicant "A" with either Guide Dog "B", "C" or "D". Whilst it is true that any one of these dogs may be more interested in farm animals than the late Guide Dog "A", and in addition they have not been trained, in a concentrated way, to deal with country roads, nonetheless negative reinforcement modified by appropriate praise emanating from the blind handler should counteract the dog's tendency to be distracted by farm animals. Also, familiarisation over a period of time will help in this matter, just as habituation to country roads will alleviate any faults in that direction. But this is to describe an extreme case. Often enough, all guide dogs will not be too distracted by farm animals, and furthermore the astute guide dog trainer will condition his dog to meet all contingencies, urban and rural alike. So the situation does not arise. Applicant "A" would have been equally suited in the final analysis to Guide Dogs "A", "B", "C" or "D", all of which, incidentally, might be yellow Labradors, but might just as well be a mix of breeds.

To further underline guide dog versatility, it should be mentioned that most guide dog trainers preparing for a class of students (in which case he will train four or five blind people in the use and care of their allocated dogs) hold an extra dog or two should things go wrong; if a dog dies or becomes ill, for instance, or if a mis-match occurs.

The commonest cause given for a mis-match is that of incompatibility of student and dog. The term incompatibility covers a multitude of sins, and at its simplest it is that the blind person just does not like, and does not get on with, the particular dog assigned to him. It might be difficult to put a finger on the exact reason for this dislike. Indeed, it may be some intangible that is totally inexplicable. Yet, call in a reserve dog and recruit it to replace the mis-matched animal and, presto, the two click straightaway. Let it be said however, that there is still the possibility that the replacement pairing will not get on together either (it is invariably the human who errs in this matter of like and dislike), in which case the blind person will return home without a dog. Whether or not he will come back at a later date to try for another dog rests with both himself and, not unnaturally, the receptivity of the guide dog school. Coincidentally, since many reserve dogs stepping into the place of an initial allottee prove to be successful, we can see that matching particular dog to particular student allows for much leeway. To counter-claim this, however, who is to say that the resultant guide dog unit would not be so much more efficient, safer and aesthetically pleasing than an original, optimal match?

As to the reasons why a student decides to give up his allocated dog during team training (thus indicating in his opinion a mis-match) it might be difficult to pinpoint such factors, be they few or many, and which might be emotional or physical, such as dissatisfaction with the trend of training, or non-gratification of mobility needs as the student views them. Perhaps there is conflict between blind person and trainer, or unrealised student achievement goals in the short-term (coupled with inability to foresee the long-term dividends which may and often result some months later as the unit blends into a workmanlike team); dislike of the school's regime; an inner conviction that the dog is not performing as it should be because of a canine temperamental fault or inadequate training; and, finally, that indeterminate circumstance, incompatibility with the allocated dog. These, and permutations of these, and a host of other reasons besides, might be accountable for the two per cent dropout rate of guide dog students in residential training. These negative features are, fortuitously, far and away outweighed - as evidenced by the 98 percent success rate - by powerful positive motivating influences so that graduation is accomplished and subsequent life-style and mobility skills enhanced.

As an example of one dropout, the finger may be placed implicitly upon one particular cause by examining the progress of an original class of eight students recently at the Bolton, England, training centre of the Guide Dogs for the Blind Association. After the assignation of dogs to students, and the elapse of some two weeks training, we begin to detect the first few notes of dissatisfaction from one member of the class who complains that his dog is smaller than the animals allocated to the other students, yet he is taller than his fellow pupils. The culmination of these feelings of disenchantment results in this particular gentleman returning home without a guide dog.

The compelling reason, surprisingly perhaps (although the student may have rightly felt that the short stature of his dog caused an imbalance, thus impeding, to some extent, effective mobility. Or he might equally have felt that the imbalance, to the onlooker, was aesthetically displeasing; perhaps even his own ego suffered somewhat through using what he considered to be a dog too small for him, especially when compared to other canines in the class) appears to be the student's discontent with his dog because it was not big enough for him. Due to this ineradicable emotion, and in common with most mis-matches, he was unable to give himself over to the dog unstintingly, and so the unit was doomed to failure at the outset.

For successful training, the student must direct himself with complete approbation to his dog in all aspects of endeavour, or otherwise the animal will be unable to perform as it should and shoddy work will result. Without this compelling vindication of student towards dog, the class trainer's efforts in favourably concluding the training of this particular unit will similarly be of little avail.

When matching a blind person to a dog, the potential capacity for control over the animal by the new owner needs to be taken into consideration. A big, burly, 'hard' (not very sensitive, and therefore needing effective physical correction when wayward) animal would presumably be allocated to a big, burly man. But this would apply only if the chap in question could maintain masterly control over the dog. Some big, burly men are in actual fact quite gentle people, and thus (whilst a big, burly dog would still be called for) a 'soft' dog (a sensitive animal needing only the minimum of physical correction) might well apply in this case. This latter dog would, of course, all other things being equal, be similarly well-suited to a large, burly woman.

The importance of stature is noted when matching dog to person, particularly when, from the example quoted, it may make the difference between success or failure, bearing in mind the fact that this was an exceptional case. Nevertheless, to afford balance to the unit, to give an added sense of security to the handler, and from the aesthetic point of view, it is wise for the tall person to be allocated with a correspondingly tall dog, a short person with a short dog (too big a dog for a short person can also create imbalance and antithesis), a heavy person with a well-built dog and (although not so important) a slight person with a slight dog. We would also hope to have a dog of brisk walking speed (allowing for effectiveness of speed control, which is part of the training curriculum) for a confident and quick-footed person, whilst the slower dog would go to the more leisurely paced (usually older) individual.

Physique and movement are thus seen to be two important factors when pairing guide dog and blind person. If, however, the blind person suffers from an additional bodily handicap, then this dysfunction will also have to be taken into account. An abnormality of gait or posture, for instance. A man with an artificial leg, a woman with a paralysed arm, a person with reduced muscular activity. Features such as these must be allowed for when preparing a dog for such a particular person. Some weeks previously, the trainer should begin to simulate the mannerisms and characteristics of the person for whom the dog is earmarked. He should walk with the animal in a clumsy fashion; he should be stiff-legged; he should stumble over kerbs; he should not use one of his arms to maintain control; he should not be as flexible in movement as he might normally be; he should collide and buffet into the dog (this animal should be of low body sensitivity and easily controlled). In short, he should be everything the potential, additionally-handicapped guide dog user will be. At the same time the canine should be responsive to correction (more especially verbal correction since the prescribed low body sensitivity will possibly render the dog less tractable to physical correction) and it should be a dog of good concentration, positive in movement, and blessed with initiative.

When matching dog to person emphasis is laid upon the temperamental aspects involved. Whilst in a number of instances these need to be taken into account, it is unwise to place too much stress upon such matters. And when temperament is taken into consideration, it is at a quite fundamental level. Since dogs vary (although guide dogs should not differ radically so) one from the other, it is a fact that dogs are trained as guides which exhibit unalike degrees of serenity and emotional balance, and are therefore presented in planes of behavioural traits, whether negative or positive, which are not constant.

We would hope that all guide dogs are placid, steady, precise animals of consistent concentration, ignorant of people about them whilst working with their blind owner, to whom their responses are unreservedly directed. We would hope also that their standard of training is such that little is left to be desired, and that their willingness for work is at a constantly high level. We would further hope that they are clean, biddable animals, socialized to such an extent that their behaviour in all societal situations is impeccable, and that their degree of habituation to our sophisticated environment leaves them unruffled and adequate no matter the complexity of circumstance, or compelling the crisis.

We would additionally hope that guide dogs are good-looking, healthy specimens (no matter of which pure breed or hybrid) of a well–proportioned physique, and where the interests and wishes of the master are placed before its own. We would hope that the dog is sufficiently conditioned to respond to the dictates of the user when speed control applies. That is to say, the dog should walk, with a good bearing, at the pace which is comfortable to the handler. We would hope that the dog is disinterested in other animals and people, and in the sights, sounds and scents which might beset it during its daily tasks as a guide. In short, to paraphrase Robert Whittington, "As time requireth.... a dog for all seasons".

Given the animal described, the matching process becomes infinitely more simple. But dogs which fulfil all the afore-mentioned requirements are thin on the ground. Therefore, when a dog of an excitable disposition is allocated, it will need to go to a calm and placid person who can assume authority over this animal to curb its impetuosity. If, however, we have an easily agitated blind man, then he in his turn must have a dog which is of a totally unruffled nature, calm to the point of indifference. However, far better for all guide dogs to be placid and easy-going and confident in action and movement and temperamentally sound so that such a dog can be assigned to both the former and the latter examples of a blind person.

A dog which might become wayward will again need to go to an authoritarian figure, whilst the easily-controlled, responsive dog must go to the indecisive type of person who exhibits inadequate tendencies in the assumption of physical and verbal dog-handling skills.

137

A person who lives and works under extraordinary conditions will require a dog which has been socialized and habituated to react favourably in such conditions. A person lacking in capacity for control necessitates a responsive dog of sound concentration and unfluctuating willingness, with a fairly high level of sensitivity – a 'soft' dog which reacts promptly to only a slight physical and verbal correction that might be ineffective to a 'harder' animal. A person having a light hold on the harness handle (the connecting link between man and dog) but who follows the dog conscientiously and sympathetically would likewise be preferred for the 'softer' dog, whilst the heavy-handed individual who follows discordantly and is slow to change course will need a positive sort of dog of lower sensitivity. And where a person with a hearing defect is trained, this will necessitate a safe, cautious animal with a high degree of initiative.

Having examined these varied facets which are taken into account before finally matching a guide dog to a blind person, and noting also the extremes in characteristics displayed by man and (but to a lower and lesser extent) canine, it takes little imagination to appreciate the many permutations and complexities of temperament and physique that can be revealed when the pairing process is considered. This is so because not just one particular trait might be exhibited by the blind student, but rather a combination of negative and positive qualities. This does not make the task of the trainer any easier when deciding on guide dog allocation. However, whilst accepting the apparent complicacy of the matching decision, the guide dog organisation and the individual trainers concerned must keep their feet planted firmly on the ground and confine the pairing process to simple, factual levels, rather than become embroiled in abstract thinking when a fundamentally physical match is about to take place.

─── *13* ───

TRAINING THE TEAM

When guide dog training is completed to satisfactory standards, the trainer who has handled the animal must now pass on his training skills to the blind person to whom the dog is to be allocated. Without effective handling of the guide dog by the blind person, inevitably the quality of work exhibited by the unit will gradually deteriorate as time goes on and poorly reinforced responses dwindle.

To state the obvious, other than the fact that the blind person cannot see, he is just like any other individual. However, depending upon the circumstances (accident, disease) which brought about his blindness, and depending upon the time of onset of visual loss (childhood; middle age) this may - but may not – affect his physical well-being and emotional maturity. For instance, a congenitally blinded individual - but not excepting a person blinded later in life - *may* display postural peculiarities, and unusual characteristics of gait, and weaknesses in grip and limb co-ordination, which *might* make handling and walking with a guide dog a little more difficult for this particular person to manage. In turn, increasing demands will be make upon the trainer concerned if he is to successfully conclude a course of training with such an individual.

Similarly with regard to emotional maturity. A blind person coming from an over-protected environment, where his parents and other relatives and friends have shielded him and discouraged development of initiative, self-care and independence, may through no fault of his own lack the motivation, determination and drive to competently cope with a guide dog.

In order to reduce, if not totally obviate, the spectre of failure, the wise trainer will visit the blind person who applies for a guide dog before deciding to undertake the task of training him. If the trainer feels that the applicant is too old and feeble (the two are not necessarily synonomous, since an elderly person may well make a suitable candidate), or too physically incapable, or lacks the necessary sense of purpose, or is not mentally sound, or cannot provide the right surroundings in which to keep a dog (although often enough in such rare circumstances a little effort on the part of both parties can put such environmental, and indeed possibly some of the other matters, right), or for some other compelling reason, then it may regrettably be that the application will be turned down. However, the trainer should naturally endeavour to keep blocks to guide dog training for a particular individual at a minimum, especially where motivation is high. Nevertheless, it is unwise to accept for training a blind person who indicates obvious signs of potential failure with a guide dog.

Three to four weeks is felt to be the optimal length of time to train a blind person and guide dog successfully together to form a workmanlike unit. It may be that a competent and quick–learning student, perhaps (but not only) one who has had a dog before, can be trained in a shorter period; two weeks, or even less, would suffice in instances where individual ability is evident. Decisions as to whether to train a group of people together, as a formal class, in a residential setting, or to teach applicants individually on a domiciliary basis, will obviously depend on the *modus operandi* of the particular trainer concerned, or rather, on the agency he works for.

Whichever setting is chosen, the methodology of training man and dog together remains much the same. Before the dog is assigned to the student, he is shown the accoutrements which accompany the animal when it is used as a guide, viz., harness, handle, lead and choke-chain; also, he is issued with a leather play collar (with small bell affixed) which is worn when the dog is running free (and indeed may be left on the animal permanently), and grooming brush and comb. The tinkling of the bell on the play collar helps indicate to the owner the whereabouts of the dog when it is enjoying free exercise. If worn whilst working, the noise of the bell can draw the attention of passers-by to the presence of a guide dog unit so that, if blocking the pavement as a group, they may step aside and not be a hindrance to the team.

The fixtures supplied with a guide dog very slightly from country to country. In Britain, the leather harness is coloured white and consists of a girth strap, with both an easy fastening clip and a stop buckle which joins underneath the dog, and a chest pad with side straps which fasten at two points each side of the girth strap. On top of the girth strap are two D-rings, wherein are clipped the hooks of the open end of the U-shaped rigid metal handle.

In the United States and Australia, and most other countries, the harness is left in its natural tan colour. Its design is simpler and stouter, comprising only girth strap and chest piece with no side straps, although sometimes integrating a surcingle. The handle is more inflexible - although still allowing a little play - and permanently affixed to the harness, unlike the British model which can be unclipped. The leather lead, with a D-ring and a clip at each extremity, to be shortened or lengthened as required (short lead when working in harness, and long lead when being allowed a modicum of freedom out of harness - but still under control since the handler retains the rein in fields or park), and metal choke-chain (or check-chain), which are used in conjunction with the harness and handle whilst working with a guide dog, are much the same world-wide.

The British handle appears in two different shapes. One straight, the other with a symmetrical off-set curve in the middle. The off-set handle is employed where a guide dog is on the sensitive side, or has a tendency to move over to the left, perhaps to avoid an indifferent handler. Where the owner might not be as deft at following as he should, the wider gap between man and dog which this curved handle affords gives the animal more leeway to move to the right when need demands it, at the same time lessening the risk of having the blind person bundling into it whilst it so manoeuvres.

Because the dog works on the left of the handler, the choke-chain must be slipped over the animal's head so that the loop passes under the dog's neck and terminates on the right. In this way, following a sharp physical correction on the lead, the choke–chain (which is allowed two or three inches of play at the extremity which joins the lead) instantly falls slack once more. If the choke-chain were to be affixed incorrectly with the loop over the top of the dog's neck it might not release readily after a correction.

The first day's training is spent in showing the student how to fix the collar, lead and harness onto his dog (for this purpose it is helpful to use a life-sized model dog), as well as practising verbal techniques relevant to developing and maintaining a rewarding relationship with a guide dog. The student thus has to broaden his talent insofar as judicious usage of the voice is concerned; he must learn to vary verbal expression to impart command, authority, pleasure and displeasure. Human utterances play such a vital part in guide dog training that it is imperative for the blind person to develop them to the pitch where appropriate responses are evoked from the dog whenever it hears its master's voice. A dull, dreary, monotonous tone will only encourage the dog to ignore, indeed be oblivious of, such a painful sound. Variety in the voice when introduced at opportune moments will serve to capture the animal's interest and attention. If the dog makes a mistake, or is distracted by another animal, a cat perhaps, then a few harsh words, if aptly applied, will work wonders. And when the dog does well, words of warmth will set the tail wagging. Praise for canine performance carried out willingly and effectively, and verbal admonition for slackness, each applied consistently and appropriately, is the message the trainer puts over to the student.

141

During this initiating day of instruction, the student is taught how to position himself in relation to the dog both whilst walking and when at a stand-still. In these two instances the handler, with the dog on his left, is alongside its hindquarters; the left arm (in training jargon, the handle arm) is kept straight by the side (not bent at the elbow) and the harness–handle is held loosely but securely - not gripped - in the upturned fingers of the left hand, palm facing backwards. Additionally, held in this hand is the lead, betwixt the fingers which enfold the handle grip.

The words of command are now practised, and the student is impressed with the need to impart injunctions with compelling authority. In order that the trainer may precisely monitor proceedings during these early stages, he himself takes the part of the dog by holding the harness extremity of the handle, whilst the blind person holds the opposite end as he will when handling the dog. The student issues the words of command and the trainer responds appropriately - if he feels the injunction to be constraining enough! "Forward", a clear, concise, expressive word, and off the trainer moves, first checking that the student is facing straight ahead and standing erect, and that he sets off smoothly and harmoniously whilst maintaining the correct walking position as he follows the 'dog' when the order is responded to.

Further commands to be mastered, with the trainer still in the canine role, during the first two days of training, are "Stop", "Back", "Right" and "Left". The student continues to be encouraged to use utterances denoting authority, and to position himself correctly in relation to the dog at all times. By becoming adept at handling a simulated dog, the student is better able to manage the actual animal when it is shortly allocated to him. And since the blind person has acquired some measure of skill and dexterity in handling techniques and positioning and voice procedure, the dog faces less trauma and mis-management than it might otherwise have met up with at the hands of a bungling and unversed novice. The value of having the trainer play the part of the dog is these early stages of instruction is thus evident.

When the trainer is happy that the student is well acquainted with the words of command used, with the correct positioning of person in relation to dog, both when moving and stationary, with the importance of voice control, and with the affixing and removing of harness, collar and lead, then the instructor will now be finalising matching, and making preparations to hand the new guide dog over to the student.

The inceptive meeting of man and dog provides a rather emotional moment for both the blind person, and, perhaps, although to a lesser extent, the trainer concerned. It is, after all, quite a milestone in the student's life, which, since his initial application, has taken a few months to arrive at this momentous occasion, where he is presented with an individually selected guide dog which is, hopefully, going to make a tremendous difference to his mobility potential. Indeed, to his way of life.

In a class situation, the students, as a group, are told their allotted dogs' names, breeds and descriptions, and then they repair to their bedrooms. Here, they anxiously await the arrival of their new dogs, brought to them on leads, by the trainer, with both human and canine hearts beating a little faster, since the dogs, now that their routine is suddenly changed, sense something a little different in the air.

The door of the bedroom is opened, following a forewarning knock, and an excited dog, kept in check by a placating trainer, tugs exuberantly on the lead across the room to meet its new owner, who, sitting at his bedside, awaits with outstretched arms and welcoming words, to have the greeting reciprocated, invariably, with a warm lick and a cold nose thrust into the palm of the hand. Being friendly animals, they are delighted to meet this stranger, who is prepared to kneel down beside them with loving caresses and affectionate words.

The trainer retires from the room, and leaves the two together for half-an-hour so that they can get to know one another on a mutual, friendly basis before, with the progression of team training, the man assumes predominance in his proper place, not just as a companion, but as a master, whilst the dog settles into its subservient yet rewarding role as a guide, responsive always to the wishes and dictates of the pack-leader.

It has been intimated to the student that whilst his dog has been allocated to him only after much deliberation regarding suitability, and that this animal is considered to be the most appropriate canine partner for him, nevertheless there is the remote possibility that if the match does not appear to be gelling as it should during the ensuing month, the trainer may feel that it would be in the best interests of the blind person if the first choice dog were to be replaced by one of the reserve animals. This eventuality, however, seldom occurs. The first choice dog is invariably the right selection, and at the end of the course of training the animal and fixtures become the property of the blind person, subject, by written agreement, to certain safeguards, viz., the dog must not be uncared for or ill-treated, reasonable access must be allowed the agency representative for purposes of after-care and canine welfare, and the animal must not be used for mendicancy or showing or pursuances other than those of guide and companion.

From the moment the dog is handed over to the student, he is now responsible, under the professional gaze and gradually diminishing practical help of trainer and kennel staff, for its care and welfare as well as its performance as a guide. The blind person assumes authority for feeding and watering the dogs once guidance is given regarding diet (usually one daily meal suffices) and grooming and exercising the animal, as well as abiding by the routine and rigid training regime which he must follow at the behest of the trainer. The student will therefore be expected to appear promptly with his dog at the specified, mainly regular, times at the parking lot within the training centre grounds where he will embark onto the mini-bus ready for the ride to the start of the morning's or afternoon's training walk. Where domiciliary, as opposed to residential, instruction is being undertaken, obviously the routine and regime will be adapted by the individual trainer to suit the home-based student and his surroundings.

When in residence, the student will have the dog with him, often enough, in the building. As circumstances deem it, the dog may be left alone, in its basket, in the student's bedroom. It will sleep in the room with him at night, and will accompany him to the dining room at meal times, to where it will be expected, after one or two days of familiarity, to guide him, whether on lead or harness, to his particular chair, and then lie quietly under the table whilst its new owner enjoys an uninterrupted meal with his fellow-students and the training and kennel personnel.

In order to re-affirm handling capabilities, even during ensuing training the instructor may have recourse to occasionally again take the part of the dog in order to demonstrate to the student a particular skill. Physical control, for instance, where the student will be shown how, when the dog is acutely distracted and not responding to verbal chastisement, to take the lead in the right hand and with a quick, strong jerk (not a prolonged pull) give a sharp correction, forcibly enough to stop the dog being wayward, bearing in mind body sensitivity. As the dog resumes concentrating on the work in hand, correction is replaced immediately by verbal praise for so doing.

To facilitate a smooth change of hand when jurisdiction over the dog is switched from one person to another, and so that the student may progressively improve his handling skills in a spiral upwards from beginner to expert, the standard of training walks correspondingly advances from simple to complex.

The introductory walks of the unit are still very much under the control of the trainer. In fact the first few sessions are stringently dominated by the trainer to the extent that, as the unit of guide dog and blind person proceeds along the pavement, the instructor still retains a long lead which is attached to the dog so that, if things go wrong, he may interpose at the crucial moment to ensure that mistakes are either not made, or do not go unpunished, and in so doing demonstrate to the student the appropriate procedures to adopt and measures to take when particular circumstances present themselves. It is rather like learning to drive. At the outset, the car is still very much in hands of the instructor driver, but as skills and handling abilities are refined the learner driver increasingly assumes control over the vehicle, yet the instructor can intervene if a crisis occurs.

Common mistakes which might crop up as the change of hand from trainer to student is being wrought during the incipient days of team training include the dog over-shooting the down-kerb (in which case the trainer instantly intervenes and compels the animal to stop by a flick of the lead); the dog not responding to right shoulder work as it should, in which instance again the trainer will ensure that the animal does perform as it must; a waning of willingness, to counteract which the handler should introduce a more encouraging and exciting tone into his voice, and be more animated in action. More variety in the training walks, with a specific destination in view, can also help overcome a drop in canine willingness to work.

During the rather confusing, albeit brief, period when the dog is transferring its allegiance from one master to another, the animal may give way to distraction in situations where previously it kept its concentration - correction will correspondingly be applied. Canine propensity for dealing with traffic and obstacles may also be adversely affected at this change-over time.

In the face of such troublesome events, which usually occur due to the temporary (but not total) breakdown of responses which have been brought about because of the altered situation and subsequent conditions (viz., the change of hand between trainer and student and the resulting consequences - for the time being – of incomplete, disparate or missing reinforcement) the trainer will add any needed impetus to ensure that the responses expected of the dog continue to be forthcoming.

However, with each succeeding walk the trainer will be asking the student to gradually and increasingly take over control of the dog, and apply reinforcement himself as and when necessary, whilst the instructor more and more disappears into the background with every passing day. So much so that the second lead attached to the dog, and retained by the trainer to help the novice handler maintain canine control, can now be dispensed with, and the walks made progressively more difficult.

The introductory and first few following walks should be performed under undemanding circumstances. They are best confined to a long, straight stretch of wide, uncluttered pavement, so that within relatively easy conditions the dog and student can get to know each other as working partners without having too much to do, or occupy their minds, during these early, formative stages. Such outings can be restricted to practising walking correctly at a comfortable pace, with emphasis on good and precise positioning (walking alongside the dog's right hindquarters, head and body erect, handle arm straight by the side but yet not rigid, and wrist flexible while the handle is held loosely but securely in the upturned fingers of the backward facing left hand) and relaxed, confident attitude.

At odd intervals the student can halt the dog by issuing a sharp command "Stop" (supplemented by a deft flick on the harness–handle if there is not a prompt response) and, after a pause of a few moments, giving the injunction "Forward", again in a voice which imparts authority. If not responded to readily, the trainer (later, the student himself) will physically induce the dog to move by jerking the long lead which he is retaining. "Back" also can be practised, but it will not be until a little afterwards that the other directional commands of "Left" and "Right" are introduced.

And so, compressed into the space of some three weeks (for the average student) is the complete range of training which the instructor himself has previously undertaken over a span of four months or so, in order to bring the dog up to class standard from being an uninitiated animal. Since the dog is now trained (albeit it may falter a little because of the changed circumstances in which it now finds itself) and the student is a rational human being who himself soon assimilates instruction, a good quality performance can reasonably be expected from the unit upon conclusion of training.

Progressing in slow but ever more advanced stages, the trainer instructs the student to handle the dog in much the same way as he himself handled it previously. He imparts his knowledge to the student in a basic and easy to understand manner, and fully enough, eventually, to cover every contingency - as far as that is possible. Lessons, both theoretical and practical, are repeated *ad infinitum* if so requested or required.

The aspect of safety is emphasised constantly during team training. It would bear ill of a guide dog owner to be foolhardy and attempt to traverse dangerous crossings without taking extreme precautions. Therefore the trainer is at pains to stress the need for extra care when his students are preparing to give the command "Forward" to their dogs at the down-kerb. The injunction should not be delivered too forcefully. Now that the dog is becoming more acquainted with the student's voice and verbal modulations, commands and reprimands are correspondingly moderated. With time and familiarity and ensuing canine response to the once strange voice of the new handler, the guide dog owner may become so temperate with his words that he will speak with barely a whisper. And the whisper will be responded to. The command "Forward" is a misnomer. It is, rather, an invitation. An invitation to the dog to cross the road when it is safe to do so. Indeed, if the 'invitation' is delivered too forcefully, in obeisance to the master the dog may feel obliged to respond regardless of the consequences.

Of course, not only guide dog owners and their trainers are preoccupied with safety. As we shall discuss shortly, no matter which mobility aid a blind person makes use of, the call for caution when embarking upon a street crossing should always be borne in mind. The experienced guide dog owner, however, is in the enviable position of enjoying an aid to mobility which shares with him, albeit unknowingly, some responsibility for undertaking the crossing safely. The handler bears in mind, however, that it is he who ultimately accepts accountability for inchoating the move.

* * * *

The safest way for a blind person to cross a road is with a sighted companion as a guide. Even then, the method is not foolproof, as witness the many sighted people who are knocked over on the roads of Britain each year. But the number of blind people with sighted escorts who get run over must be almost nil. The fact that they are now responsible for the safety of another individual encourages a sighted guide to be doubly careful whilst undertaking a road crossing.

Sighted assistance is, however, not always at hand, and the blind person travelling alone must perforce engage upon road crossings solo. On quieter roads a blind pedestrian, with or without a guide dog, may be quite capable and confident enough to enter into the task on his own.

The rules for road safety apply as much to the blind as they do to the sighted. The advice handed out to the sighted public by the Royal Society for the Prevention of Accidents (RoSPA) is equally applicable to the blind. Sighted people are so much in need of road safety instruction in this sophisticated world of ours that the Department of Transport spends millions of pounds each year in disseminating advice through the media of television, radio, cinema, lectures, press and publicity handouts in order to enlighten them with regard to road crossing procedures.

The simple guidelines propounded by the road safety people are to be followed by all and sundry, whether blind or sighted, and, if the former, no matter which mobility aid is used. On this principle, therefore, when a road crossing is envisaged a blind person should, first of all, and if in reasonable proximity, use a footbridge or subway. It is well worth-while making a detour to reach a safe crossing point. A couple of hundred metres added to the length of a journey is adequately recompensed if the extra distance entailed brings you to a Pelican crossing or a pedestrian subway. A blind person will make himself familiar with the geography of his home area to the extent that all safe road crossing points are well-known and used to advantage. There are, nevertheless, those roads which have to be crossed and where there are no man-made facilities to make the crossing easier or safer. It is in these situations that a blind person will need to exercise his mobility skills at a constantly high level.

Rule one in road safety is: "First find a safe place to cross, and then stop." Safe crossing places include subways, footbridges, zebra and Pelican crossings, traffic lights, and points where there is a policeman or traffic warden. Failing all these, a road junction would be the next most advantageous place to cross. It is worth bearing in mind that the Department of Transport Driving Manual states explicitly that "When turning into a road junction motorists should give way to pedestrians who are crossing the road."

Where it is impossible to involve one or more of the desirable characteristics outlined when crossing the street is envisaged, great care will need to be exercised to find a clear stretch of road free of parked cars. Since vehicles aren't allowed to park at road junctions, this is obviously another factor in favour of such a location.

Parked cars prove to be points of danger because (a), the pedestrian is obscured from view to passing motorists; (b), whether the blind person about to cross the road is a guide dog owner or not, his hearing receptivity and localization will be lessened by the interference of the adjacent parked car; (c), if a guide dog unit moves off to cross a road between parked cars, the chances of the guide dog stopping for moving traffic further out into the road are dramatically reduced, and (d), parked cars can prove to be obstacles requiring careful negotiation before leaving the down-kerb, and on regaining the up-kerb on the opposite side of the road. Such obstacles will also prevent straight crossings, which are so important to blind people, and more especially guide dog owners. An additional hazard presented by parked vehicles might be the projecting tailboards of lorries and the like, with which chest or head can come into unwelcome contact.

Road safety rule two, whether crossing at road junctions or not, is: "Stand on the pavement near the kerb." This does not mean standing on the very edge of the kerb, for traffic frequently comes in closer than one might expect. On wet days the risk of a cold shower as vehicles pass through puddles is diminished if the pedestrian stands a little away from the edge. And, much more important, the mischance of nasal abrasions (for the dog or for the human) is similarly lessened. In particular, a pedestrian at the pavement edge of a road junction is placed in a position of danger by vehicles - especially articulated lorries - whose rear wheels mount the kerb edge in order to negotiate a turning into the intersecting road. Such lorry drivers often leave it to the initiative of the pedestrian to step back and allow him room to manoeuvre his vehicle. It is important, therefore, that blind persons, whether cane travellers or guide dog users, choose a place to stand that is neither too near to the pavement edge nor too far from it. The busy market towns of Britain, with their narrow pavements and roads, provide many such potentially vulnerable situations. At such junctions, the cane traveller should prominently display his white stick, and the guide dog user might find it beneficial to carry a similar artefact whilst still at the down-kerb. This helps the motorist to identify him as a blind person and allow extra leeway while turning his vehicle. The paws of the guide dog should therefore not hang over the pavement edge, nor should the long cane or white stick be planted in the gutter.

The dog or stick, at susceptible and busy corners, should be about a foot away from the down-kerb. And the blind pedestrian should be at the ready to step back if he suspects a turning vehicle - especially a large one - is about to pass a little too close for comfort.

The journeys of cane travellers and guide dog users will be such that, fortuitously, the crossings most frequently encountered will be those involving road junctions. And the road junction to contend with most often will be the simple T-junction where a minor road meets a major road at - more or less - a right angle, and the crossing entailed is that of the minor road. With the blind traveller maintaining a straight path along the pavement, and where the corner is sharply right-angled (as opposed to a gradually rounded corner - sometimes loosely referred to as a gradually rounded kerb), the approach to the down-kerb is completed so that when the pedestrian stops at the kerb, he is facing directly across the road and thus projecting himself towards the opposite up-kerb. This projection keeps him on a straight line as he crosses the road and proceeds safely along the pavement at its recommencement. The din of parallel traffic along the major road also helps him to effect a straight crossing across the minor road.

Complications can arise, however, where the road junction is not so clearly defined, and where the corners, rather than being right-angled, are gradually rounded. If a straight approach to a gradually rounded corner is made, to be followed by a straight crossing, it will be noted (Figure 7-2) that the crossing is uncommonly wide - so much so that four lanes of traffic might be encountered rather than the more usual two. To counteract this, the pedestrian should make an indentation round the corner to a point where the road crossing is considerably narrower. Fortunately, most local authorities, in their wisdom, have placed guard rails round the busier corners on road junctions so that the pedestrian is obliged, whether he likes it or not, to approach the gap in the rails where the road to be crossed is at its narrowest. At less busy junctions, however, such guard rails might not be present, but an indentation should still be made. The guide dog owner will find that his dog has been trained to indent at gradually rounded corners, a procedure which should be encouraged and maintained by the handler. When a straight crossing has been made, a counter-indentation will, of course, need to be made on the up-kerb to avoid the building line (Figure 7-2). And as shown in Figure 13-1, similar indentations and counter-indentations will need to be made at roundabouts which, as far as the guide dog unit is concerned, are simply gradually rounded corners on a grander scale.

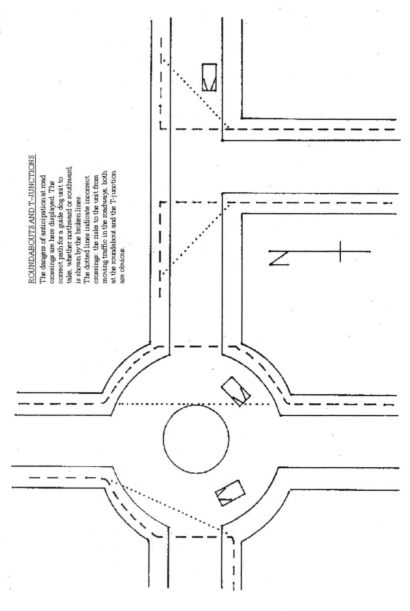

Figure 13-1

ROUNDABOUTS AND T-JUNCTIONS

The dangers of anticipation at road crossings are here displayed. The correct path for a guide dog unit to take, whether northward or southward is shown by the broken lines.
The dotted lines indicate incorrect crossings: the risks to the unit from moving traffic in the roadways, both at the roundabout and the T-junction are obvious.

150

A similar indentation will be made by the long cane user. It should be mentioned that even on sharply right-angled corners and where the blind pedestrian is unsure of making a straight crossing, the long cane traveller will indent so as to ensure reaching the opposite up-kerb. If a blind person's locational sense and spatial appreciation is such that a straight line is difficult to maintain, then there is a possibility that he will cross the road at an angle and miss the up-kerb, thus exposing himself to danger from traffic on the main road. Alternatively, he will wander much too far down the minor road. This is the advantage of a good guide dog, which will keep its owner on a true course. An inferior dog with an unsure handler might, however, make the same mistakes as a disorientated cane traveller.

Guide dog units will approach the down-kerb to a right-angled corner in a straight line and effect a straight crossing. It should be borne in mind, however, that where a guide dog, because of previous experience, is expecting a turn on the up-kerb it may begin to anticipate this, with the effect that the road is crossed diagonally - an undesirable tendency (see Figure 13-1) that must be corrected by the handler.

To avoid diagonal crossings and time spent dallying dangerously in the parallel road, the blind traveller will need also to indent or (depending upon direction of travel) counter-indent at down-kerbs and up-kerbs with off-set corners as shown in Figure 7-2. The object of the exercise is to effect a straight crossing over the intersecting road, and only an indentation or counter–indentation can bring this about.

Having arrived at the down-kerb, and having positioned himself correctly after, if need be, an appropriate indentation, the blind pedestrian will now implement rule three of road safety procedure: "Listen for traffic." It should be noted that traffic may be coming from all manner of directions depending upon particular road layouts and traffic flow systems.

Now to be effected is rule four: "If traffic is coming, let it pass, then listen again." If fast traffic is approaching, or any moving vehicles are near, wait for it to pass. When unsure, always let traffic pass and then continue listening carefully to make sure that no other vehicles are coming. If one lot of traffic has gone past, it doesn't mean there won't be any more, particularly since the sound of traffic recently passed can obscure the noise of following vehicles. Rule five, then, is: "When there is no traffic near, walk straight across the road." It is presumed safe to cross when there is no traffic near. If there is traffic in the distance, the pedestrian should not cross unless absolutely sure there is plenty of time. Then he should walk straight across the road, but without hurrying.

A guide dog unit should always cross roads at a leisurely pace. This ensures that the dog can stop for any far traffic, allows the guide dog owner to maintain a comfortable and correct walking position, and reduces the possibility of tripping over the up-kerb. The guide dog owner should have a white symbol cane in his right hand during the crossing. It is essential that the motorist who suddenly arrives on the scene should be aware that the person crossing is visually impaired. The sixth and last rule of road safety is therefore exercised: "Keep listening for traffic while you cross." In the case of a guide dog unit, if it appears that the dog might continue forward even in the face of far traffic the onus will be upon the handler to make an emergency stop. Similarly, a long cane traveller will have to be perceptive enough to come to a standstill if necessary, difficult though such a procedure might be. This only serves to emphasise the need for accuracy in applying rules three and four.

To assist motorists, it is wise for the visually handicapped pedestrian to make himself conspicuous through the use not only of the white stick, but also the reflective armband. Since armbands might become obscured, however, a most useful additional device is the reflectorised Sam Browne-style combined waist and cross belt, worn by many motor cyclists to make themselves readily visible to other road users. These cross-belts are of a lightweight material that can be folded up when not in use and carried in a pocket or handbag. There is also a slipover style, popularly worn by joggers, and these valuable aids can be purchased at motor cycle and sports shops. It is good for the pedestrian to wear these distinctive devices at all times, but more especially at night. The Department of Transport exhorts people abroad during the hours of darkness to "shine out with reflective material", and points out that many serious accidents to pedestrians happen because drivers do not see people on the road until it is too late to stop. The fact is that most clothing is dark and does not show up very well from a distance in poor light. Reflective material is specially designed to become luminous when exposed to beams of light such as car headlamps, and works by reflecting the light straight back at the driver. It is comprised of thousands of tiny glass lenses that act in the same way as the 'cats' eyes' which mark traffic lanes.

On an unlit road, a driver with dipped headlights can see a pedestrian wearing reflective material at over 300 metres. If you are wearing something white, the driver will see you at about 100 metres. If you are wearing dark clothes, he will not see you - if at all - until he is less than 50 metres away. And if the motorist is driving at 50 miles an hour, on a dry road, in a car with good brakes, and has quick reactions, he will need about 60 metres to stop from the moment he sees you. On a wet road, the stopping distance might be doubled.

It should be noted that for daytime wear fluorescent material is more visible to others, whilst reflective apparel is useful at night. Fortunately, the two substances are combined in most clothing accoutrements made for road safety. Guide dog users' armbands, for instance, involve both fluorescent and reflective materials, and are thus ideal for day and darkness. Most crossbelts and slipovers also combine fluorescent day-time brightness and retro-reflective night-time brilliance. And the way some motorists drive these days, pedestrians really can't be bright enough.

*   *   *   *

The whole gamut of training covered before the student takes over the dog is encapsulated in concise but comprehensive form now that the blind person has charge of the animal and must learn to use and control it within a comparatively short space of time. Obedience, both on and off the lead, especially the recall when the dog is enjoying free exercise in park or field; social behaviour in and out-of-doors and whilst travelling on public transport (the canine should lie quietly under the table, or seat, or alongside the owner, when visiting people in their homes; not jump up at anyone; and not go looking for food from the table), in short, not make a nuisance of itself.

And then, when the dog is working in harness, the student must learn how to maintain control, to impart commands and have them responded to promptly; how to work the dog on stations, in offices and shops; how to keep to the correct position in relation to the animal whilst walking along; how to perfect kerb drill (a consistent stop by the dog, and have it remain steady at the down-kerb whilst waiting for the road to be clear); how to deal with obstacles and traffic; how to negotiate crowds of people on busy pavements, and how to hold high levels of canine performance once these standards have been built up and reached.

During class training, the unit will be expected to contend with two, but sometimes one, and now and then perhaps three, walks a day (of about 45 minutes duration), which will fit in with a pre-planned schedule covering the contingencies presented by most urban areas and - although less emphasis is placed upon this unless the student is a country dweller - rural conditions besides. The aim of the training course is for the blind person to return home with his guide dog a happy and confident individual secure in the knowledge of his ability to practise his new-found skills without the supervision of the trainer. The student will now be able to effect such control over his dog that it will abide by his wishes in any given situation, and high standards of performance will be expected from both human and canine whenever they are out together working as a team.

To monitor the quality of work as time goes on, to sort out any problems that may have arisen and to correct slack or falling standards, as well as to check the health and welfare of the canine and replace worn-out equipment, and to offer advice regarding routes and environmental hazards, it is advisable for the trainer to visit the guide dog unit in the home area at least once a year. Ideally, an after-care trip such as this should be carried out when the newly qualified team first returns home. This purpose will of course already be served in those instances where domiciliary training has preceded qualification.

14

GUIDE DOG CONTROL

The capabilities of a trained dog will only be displayed at their maximum, dependent upon the skill and aptitude of the handler. This is as true, if not more so, of the guide dog as it is in any sphere of animal training. Many blind persons beginning training with guide dogs are complete novices when it comes to handling their charges. For some, it is the first time they have owned or handled a dog. Even where a blind person has had experience of dog handling before, when being trained with a guide dog he is asked to put all previous knowledge behind him, and to consider this venture as a completely fresh and innovative start, where he will discover new skills and new approaches in the field of animal training and ownership.

Because of the need to adopt a totally different approach, for the blind person to be instructed in the methodology of guide dog work, as well as to afford an opportunity for man and dog to get to know one another whilst working under supervision, and, more important, for the man to assume the role of pack leader and the dog to accept a subordinate role, it is obviously necessary for a period of time to elapse. This is why some three or four weeks are spent by the trainer, whether in a residential class situation or a domiciliary setting, in instructing the man and dog together as a team once the initial allocation and introduction has taken place (figure 14-1).

During this comparatively short stretch of intensive training together, the blind person is taught, above all else, to control his guide dog. Without adequate control, the quality of work and subsequent performance would leave much to be desired. In all avenues of guide dog work, as well as in the domestic and social situations, the importance of canine control is constantly emphasised by the trainer instructing the novice guide dog owner.

155

Figure 14-1

THE 28-DAY CLASS TRAINING SCHEDULE		

DAY		MORNING	AFTERNOON
FRI	1	STUDENTS ARRIVE AT TRAINING CENTRE	
	2	HOUSE AND GROUNDS FAMILIARISATION. HANDLE WALKS	
SUN	3	HANDLE WALKS. ALLOCATION OF DOGS. OBEDIENCE	
	4	TWO QUIET TRAINING WALKS WITHOUT ROAD CROSSINGS	
	5	TWO TRAINING WALKS INTRODUCING QUIET CROSSINGS	
	6	TWO WALKS INVOLVING CROSSINGS	
	7	TWO WALKS ALONG BUSIER AND MORE VARIED ROUTES	
	8	HANDLE WALKS: TURNS	TRAINING WALK WITH TURNS
	9	SET ROUTE TO CAFE	SET ROUTE TO CAFE
SUN	10	TOWN WALK	AFTERNOON OFF
	11	TOWN WALK	ARTIFICIAL TRAFFIC
	12	TOWN WALK	ARTIFICIAL TRAFFIC
	13	HANDLE WALKS: OBSTACLES	ARTIFICIAL TRAFFIC
	14	ARTIFICIAL OBSTACLE WORK	WALK TO PARK FOR FREE RUN
	15	ARTIFICIAL OBSTACLE WORK	WALK TO PARK FOR FREE RUN
	16	SET ROUTE TO CAFE	COUNTRY WALK
SUN	17	RAILWAY STATION	AFTERNOON OFF
	18	RAILWAY STATION	SHOPS, ESCALATORS, LIFTS
	19	ARTIFICIAL OBSTACLE WORK	GROUP WALK
	20	ARTIFICIAL OBSTACLE WORK	GROUP WALK
	21	WALKS INVOLVING NATURAL TRAFFIC AND OBSTACLE WORK	
	22	TOWN WALKS WITH UNUSUAL JUNSTIONS. SUBWAY, STEPS, SHOPPING	
	23	SET ROUTE TO CAFE	TOWN WALK: TRAFFIC LIGHTS
SUN	24	COUNTRY WALK	AFTERNOON OFF
	25	RAILWAY STATION	BUS TRAVEL. SHOPPING PRECINCT
	26	ARTIFICIAL TRAFFIC, OBSTACLES	TOWN WALK
	27	ARTIFICIAL TRAFFIC, OBSTACLES	PHOTOGRAPHERS
	28	CONCLUDING WALK	DISCUSS ROUTES IN HOME AREAS
FRI	29	SIGN AGREEMENTS	DEPARTURE OF CLASS

Whichever trip is out training the remaining one at the
centre carries out feeding, grooming, free-running, social
behaviour indoors, and obedience work
Lectures and discussions are held on occasional evenings.

At home, the handler controls the dog by not allowing it to become a nuisance should it, for instance, pester other family members or callers, whether for attention or for food. With one firm command, "Bed", the dog is despatched instantly to its basket, where it will remain until bidden otherwise. When visiting other people's homes, or meeting people socially for business or pleasure, or out shopping or at the church, pub or theatre, the guide dog owner maintains constant and careful control over his charge by making it stay quietly at his side, or under the chair in which he is sitting, with quiet but effective words of command, so that those persons about him are hardly aware of the presence of an animal. Domestic, social and business situations all warrant this observance of impeccable behaviour on the part of the dog, under the controlling influence of the handler. If this pattern of restraint is rigidly adhered to by the owner in the early stages of the partnership, before long the dog will be responding satisfactorily to the dictates of the handler who will now need only exercise a modicum of control.

The control begins from the moment the harness is affixed to the dog. At the behest of the owner, the animal stands quietly whilst the simple body harness is fastened round its girth. It then waits until a command to move forward, or other directional signal, is given, to which it responds promptly. If indoors, it will approach the exit door to await further instructions from the handler. If outdoors, it proceeds along its way until an environmental feature, such as a down-kerb, halts it in its path, or instructed otherwise by the owner.

An untrained dog might meander along a pavement, stopping and sniffing at any choice scent which caught its fancy, or to investigate another dog, or to attempt to give chase to a cat, or to pay attention to pigeons, or to steal an ice-cream from the hand of a small child. The trained dog is taught to ignore all such distractions; it is instructed to walk relatively briskly in a straight line along the centre of the pavement with its head held high, and to concentrate on the work in hand. Only at the approach to a down-kerb or an obstacle will it stop. But the trained dog will only persist in this behaviour if it is adequately and precisely controlled by the handler whose charge it is. For good behaviour to persist, such behaviour must be positively reinforced; and for bad behaviour to be eradicated, this behaviour must be negatively reinforced. This is the basis for control.

The astute handler, therefore, when the dog performs well, praises the animal with warm words of encouragement; and when it is ill-behaved, he scolds it roundly and quickly with sharp words of derision, and through an admixture of verbal and sometimes, if the situation warrants it, physical control compels the dog to behave as it should.

157

There are few avenues of guide dog work where some measure of control is not called for. Distraction, the paying of attention by the guide dog to some outside influence instead of devoting itself undividedly to its work, springs foremost to mind. Whenever the dog appears to be distracted, the owner should therefore promptly correct the dog, and praise it only when it returns its attention to work. This control must be effected speedily and appropriately. It is no good correcting the dog *after* the source of distraction has disappeared. Correction must be administered at the moment of distraction. And correction must not be prolonged. It must be short and sharp and it must be effective, so that the dog's concentration is directed instantly to the job in hand - that of guiding a blind person.

When dominating the dog, canine sensitivity will need to be taken into account. A 'soft' dog will require only slight correction, whilst the 'hard' animal will warrant a stronger application. The handler must beware, however, of under-correcting his charge. Even in the instance of a 'soft' dog, if the corrections are so slight that little impression is make upon the animal, then as the months go by, and with repeated application of such unimpressionable control, the canine will become more resilient and resistent to such poorly applied correction, with the result that its body sensitivity will be lowered. In other words, such physical correction improperly applied below the requisite level for this particular 'soft' dog, will result in building up bodily resistance to the extent where it becomes a 'hard' dog. And if it is a 'hard' dog to start with, then over the months it will become even harder. The end result is, that in both instances, the handler will eventually find it increasingly difficult to exercise ascendancy over his dog when it is being distracted, or indeed in any other circumstance. Thus the importance of not only judicious short, sharp corrections at appropriate moments, but additionally of ensuring that these corrections are *adequate*, bearing in mind individual canine body sensitivity, to effect control.

One area of authority can be measured in terms of instant response to words of command. The handler says "Sit", and the dog sits; he says "Down", and the dog lies down; he says "Stay", and the dog stays; he says "Come", and the dog returns to hand. If any of these commands are not complied with, the handler disciplines the dog by physically compelling the animal to carry out his wishes. By so doing, in order to avoid physical and uncomfortable compulsion there is every chance that the dog will, on the next occasion, abide by the handler's request on verbal terms alone.

When working in harness, some measure of constraint is wrought by the wearing of the body fitment itself. Through repetition, and an *association of ideas,* the dog has become aware that, now it is wearing the harness, it is 'on duty'; there is work to be done; it must pay attention. Because of this 'thought' in the dog's mind, it ill-behoves the handler to view the association lightly. Therefore, as soon as the harness is affixed, the handler too, through the nature of his control of the dog, must ensure that the subsequent performance from the animal is of a high degree. And he must not treat the value of the harness, when fixed to the dog, flippantly. It would be most unwise, for instance, to leave the harness on the dog whilst it is at play.

Once a walk has been undertaken and successfully completed, and there is time now for the dog to relax at the fireside, or in its basket, or to run free in garden or park, then the harness is immediately removed, only to be put on again when a further journey is envisaged. And if the journey necessitates a fairly lengthy trip on public transport, with the dog lying under bus or train seats, again the harness is removed (this also protects the fixture from scuffing and unnecessary wear, as well as providing for the comfort of the dog) and put on again as the stop is neared, and further walking is to be undertaken. And if dropping in at a friend's house, or other port of call, and staying there for a little while, once more the harness is doffed. At every instance where work is not expected from the dog, and it may lie down, run free, or otherwise relax, then in order that the animal may retain unsullied the 'on-duty' image of the harness, and so that the controlling influence of the handler remains constant, the body fitment should be promptly removed.

All guide dogs, and all aspects of guide dog work, will, at one time or another, warrant the introduction of some measure of control by the handler. Varying dogs, however, will merit varying degrees of dominance. Compensating for this, when each individual dog is allocated to a particular person, the trainer will have taken this into account when matching man and canine together. He will ensure that a dog requiring a fair amount of control will be matched to a person who is well able to administer this control. And a dog requiring only a little restraint will go to a gentleman or lady who is lacking somewhat in a propensity for wielding authority over a guide dog. Nevertheless, control will still need to be applied on occasion even with regard to this more biddable animal. Every guide dog owner, therefore, no matter the nature of the dog assigned to him, and no matter the differing circumstances in which he finds himself whilst out with his dog will, on a number of not infrequent exigencies, need to apply effective control over his charge. Even the dog requiring little discipline whilst working, once it becomes aware that a new owner exhibits little ability in applying this modicum of control, will quite possibly become increasingly recalcitrant.

But how can a blind person know, for sure, when his dog is being distracted? Perhaps it is only moving to left or right in order to avoid an on-kerb obstacle, rather than moving towards a lamp post to sniff it, or to approach and investigate a passing dog? Through time, and practice, the nature of canine movement transmitted via the harness and handle may indicate to the increasingly experienced guide dog owner whether his dog is being distracted, or is avoiding an obstacle, and consequently discipline will be administered appropriately and accordingly. But until such time as his perception leads him to be aware of circumstances rightly, the blind person must control his dog even if he only *thinks* it is being distracted. The guide dog must be allowed, especially in these early stages, no room for error, and therefore if the handler is in doubt as to whether his dog is distracted or not, he must assume the worst and correct the animal in the appropriate manner on the grounds that it is being inattentive, even if he is unsure that it really is. The dog will hold no grudge against the handler. It is not in the nature, or within the capacity, of the dog to feel 'slighted' at unjust correction. Anyway, as a counterbalance in guide dog work, after a correction is given, and when the owner feels the desired response to be forthcoming, the animal is now warmly praised. Any 'misdemeanour' for which the animal is punished, whether justified or not, is of only fleeting duration, and work promptly resumes on an even keel to the tune of the guide dog owner's now encouraging tone of voice.

Of course, during initial training whilst the unit is working under supervision, the trainer will tell the blind person the choice moments to administer control. This in itself will help the owner, later, to determine when and where not to correct the dog for waywardness.

But distraction is only one area calling for control over the guide dog by the handler. If the dog overshoots a kerb, the handler instantly stops and brings the animal sharply, with a jerk of the lead, back behind him and then to his left to be positioned, as it originally should, at the down-kerb edge. Now it receives a word of praise, and a longer pause than usual is allowed to elapse before the command "Forward" is given.

The dog may be faulty in its right shoulder work or crowd work, and again control is merited. The animal brushes its handler's right shoulder against a post or hedge, and the owner promptly responds by an incisive verbal scolding and reminder, together with a deft leftward flick on the harness-handle which pushes the dog further over to the left, where it should have been in the first place in order to properly have the person avoid the post. Similarly, when going through crowds of people; the identical correction is given if the handler collides with a passer-by.

In obstacle work, if an off-kerb obstruction is approached and the dog makes no attempt to deviate and avoid it, the handler will be faced with the job of ensuring that the dog performs satisfactorily on such an occasion. However, previous instruction under the aegis of the trainer will help him in his task. To control the animal, if the parallel road is on the left when the unit contends with an obstacle, the dog will need to approach fairly near to the obstacle before it deviates to the down-kerb at the side.

If the dog is unsure, the handler will need to restrain the animal in such obstacle negotiation. Perhaps the dog has taken the handler so near to the obstacle that he is in contact with it; the blind person will now push the dog left with his knee and indicate the down-kerb to the animal, where it will stop and await the command to move off. To effect control, the handler may need to hold the lead lightly in the right hand, and using rapid, rightward jerks, encourage the dog around the obstacle so that it may regain the pavement at the earliest once the obstruction is negotiated.

Where the parallel road is on the right, and the guide dog owner comes into contact with an obstacle, he will need to transfer the lead to the free hand, but only to get the dog to the down-kerb, again by using light, indicative jerks to the right. Once there, he replaces the lead in the left hand, and negotiates the obstacle by, when in the roadway, slightly overtaking and pushing the dog gently but insistently towards the left so that, once again, with the obstruction safely cleared, the pavement is immediately regained.

Effecting a turn might necessitate the interception of the guide dog owner, especially where a deviation from a known route is taken. For instance, at a particular point on a journey a guide dog might be accustomed to turning left, but on this occasion the handler decides to turn right. Perhaps, from the stationary position at the down-kerb, the dog awaits the customary command "Left" from its owner, and is all prepared to move in this direction. However, the command "Right" is given. Nothing daunted, and hardly hearing the changed command, the dog moves left. The owner, however, quickly controls the situation by deftly taking the lead in the free hand and jerking it to the right, so that the dog is now obliged to move in this direction as the handler reiterates the verbal command.

In traffic work the guide dog owner must once more be in control of the situation. It may be that the handler, positioned with his dog at the down-kerb, issues the command "Forward" to the animal when it is unsafe to cross the road. The dog, however, responds and makes a move to leave the kerb, oncoming traffic notwithstanding. Swiftly and decisively the owner stops the dog in its tracks with a sharp jerk on the harness-handle, thus compelling it to stay in position at the down-kerb as he verbally admonishes the animal for endeavouring to move off when faced with danger. Restraint exercised by the guide dog owner in these circumstances must be both perceptive and apt. He must discern at very short notice the guide dog's mistake as far as traffic work is concerned, and he must instantly apply appropriate correction to counter the animal's efforts to leave the down–kerb. Thereafter, he must decide when it is safe to cross the road.

Left-bowed crossings (figure 14-2) will merit control by the handler, perhaps through the judicious use of the lead when held in the free hand, and giving light jerks to the right if the dog veers left. Often, the simple act of holding the lead lightly in the right hand will achieve the desired results.

Where a Y-junction has to be contended with, it is inopportune to cross at its widest point (figure 14-2). It is best to proceed along the arm of the junction and then turn left or right to the parallel kerb so that a right-angled optimal crossing is effected.

Figure 14-2

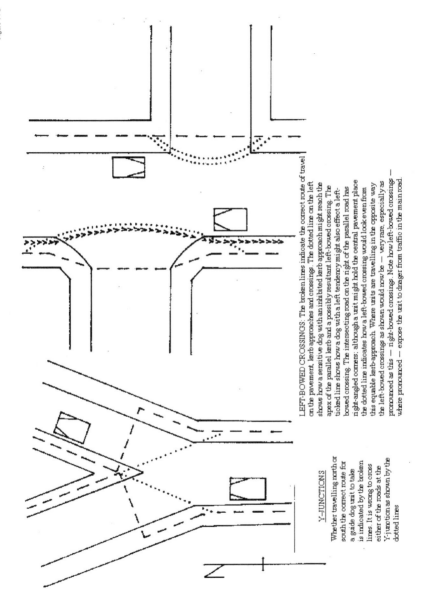

LEFT-BOWED CROSSINGS: The broken lines indicate the correct route of travel on the pavement, kerb approaches and crossings. The dotted line on the left shows how a sensitive dog with an inhibited kerb approach might reach the apex of the parallel kerb and a possibly resultant left-bowed crossing. The ticked line shows how a dog with a left tendency might also effect a left-bowed crossing. The intersecting road on the right of the parallel road has right-angled corners: although a unit might hold the central pavement place the dotted line indicates how a left-bowed crossing would look even from this equable kerb-approach. Where units are travelling in the opposite way the left-bowed crossings as shown would now be — very rare, especially as pronounced as this — right-bowed crossings. Note how left-bowed crossings — where pronounced — expose the unit to danger from traffic in the main road.

Y-JUNCTIONS

Whether travelling north or south the correct route for a guide dog unit to take is indicated by the broken lines. It is wrong to cross either of the roads at the Y-junction as shown by the dotted lines

163

Often, to clarify the situation, and to ensure a trouble-free crossing, on busy roads the guide dog owner may solicit sighted help. If this is the case, the sighted individual who is helping a blind person to cross the road should approach the guide dog owner on his right. He is thus on the side away from the dog, which is on the left. The blind person links arms with his sighted helper - the latter does not take the arm of the former- as he allows the handle to fall free on his dog's back whilst retaining the lead in his left hand. When the road is clear, the trio now make their way across, with the dog - since the handle is not being held it is consequently aware that it is not at this moment working as a guide - trotting alongside the left of its owner. The sighted helper of course tells the blind person when to step up or down at kerbs and central reservations, and, having crossed the road, now asks the guide dog owner in which direction he wishes to go in case he has become a little disorientated.

Where a guide dog owner has decided to cross a busy road without such sighted help, he will be doubly aware of the need to exercise control over his charge during the crossing. He will need to determine the pace at which the dog crosses the road, and he will need to keep the animal on a straight course as it heads for the opposite up-kerb. Most guide dogs will esure these two measures of their own volition, but where an animal decides to go too quickly, or makes a deviation during the crossing, then the handler will quickly intercede in order to correct either or both of these tendencies.

Part way across the road, traffic might appear, thus necessitating a stop in the middle of the street by the unit. Although the guide dog has been trained to stop for far traffic such as this, the owner is instructed to implement his own safety and reinforcement measures should the animal be reluctant to halt promptly to allow vehicles to proceed in front. If the owner hears far traffic in the offing, and the dog shows no signs of stopping, the person himself must stop, and constrain the canine to do likewise with a forceful downward and backward jerk on the handle together with scolding words. Only when the way is clear may the guide dog take the initiative and move off, accompanied in the correct position by the handler who now issues words of praise.

Speed control is a necessary adjunct to guide dog training since the pace of walking is set by the handler and not by the animal. If the dog tries to walk at a fast and uncomfortable pace, the owner controls the speed by plying the harness-handle up and down, thus restricting the animal in its movements, at the same time introducing a dull, monotonous, lethargic tone into his voice which implies the need for slowing down. It is wrong to try to slow a quick moving dog down by forcibly pulling against the handle. This ploy will serve only to have the dog haul even harder against the extra resistance it now feels through the harness-handle.

In those instances where the dog proceeds too slowly, the owner will now sound excited, and urge the animal to walk more quickly, perhaps shaking the harness-handle a little, or jangling the lead, and making short, running movements on the spot (but always retaining the correct position in relation to the dog - to go ahead of the animal may place the person in a position of vulnerability) so that this general air of excitement and urgency will incite the dog to progress more speedily. Where a dog is advancing slowly because of unwillingness, it is a good idea to introduce a destination to the walk where there is some form of reward for the animal. A run in the park, for instance, or a pleasant sojourn by the fireside or in the garden at a friend's house.

It will have been noted that there are few instances indeed in guide dog practice where the value of control by the handler is not merited. But the basis for such control relies upon respect of the dog for the wishes of the owner. To gain this respect the handler must assert his authority, forthrightly at times if the dog is wayward, with the requisite discreet application of both verbal and physical control, dependent upon the sensitivity of the animal. If such control is not forthcoming, or if it is frequently given at the wrong time so that the dog cannot comprehend why it is being punished, or if the degree of discipline is insufficient, then it may regrettably ensue that the quality of performance exhibited by the guide dog will fall below standard.

On the credit side, if the measure of control applied by the handler is immediate, appropriate, just and of sufficient intensity, then as time goes on the need to correct the dog will diminish. The animal, becoming aware that should it show recalcitrance the consequence will be instant correction and admonition, is less inclined to be wayward in order to avoid punishment for forbidden behaviour. So it is that the call for control can fade as the months go by, and yet standards of performance remain high. Nevertheless, the guide dog owner must be ever-vigilant, and not hesitate to reintroduce control when canine ill-behaviour demands it.

15

GUIDE DOG CARE

Compulsory intensive exercise in excessively hot, humid weather (a rarity in the British Isles) may cause heat stroke. Restricted water intake and obesity in dogs causes them to be more prone to this condition. A vehicle with a dog left in it with windows unopened and parked in an unshaded spot can be lethal to the animal within a very short space of time. Capacious tiered wire crates, as used by some American guide dog schools, well spaced out in the training van, are ideal in these extreme conditions. The dogs are not tempted to romp and play – or indeed fight - with each other, as they would if they were in an uncontrolled bunch together. Additionally, because the dogs are in these spacious, hygienic and comfortable wire crates, not only the windows of the van but both the back and side doors can be left open as each animal, in turn, awaits its training walk. In the severely hot weather which covers much of the United States in the summer months, it is most necessary to park the training van in a shaded area, under trees or alongside a high wall, taking care that the sun, as it alters position, does not leave the spot unshaded. Guide dog schools in the United States are careful in ensuring that such shade is always offered when training vans are parked. And ample water for the dogs is constantly available.

Rather than risk the potential failure to find a suitably shaded parking spot when instructors and students are training with their dogs in urban areas, the American schools also operate from 'downtown facilities' which are situated centrally in the nearest city to the main training centre. These premises are used by students, dogs and trainers during those interim periods when they are not involved in training walks. The premises have air conditioned rooms, with comfortable chairs for the students, as well as a selection of braille books and a radio and music centre. The dogs lie contentedly on the carpeted floors. If preferred, man and dog can rest in the cool, shaded verandah adjacent to the main building. Soft drinks and fresh water are available to quench human and canine thirsts.

Though Britain rarely 'suffers' such hot summers as those in the United States, nevertheless there are spells of warm weather where it would be more comfortable for the dogs if doors and windows in training vans could, when a metal grid is safely and suitably affixed, remain open. As in America, of course, trainers take painstaking precautions to ensure that vans are parked in heavily shaded areas during hot spells. And whilst in transit, windows are left wide open.

If, out training or at free exercise, a dog shows signs of heat stroke (distressed and excessive panting, staggering, collapse and perhaps unconsciousness) action to bring relief should be prompt. Immersion in a cold water bath, or hosing profusely, until the dog begins to recover, followed by rest in a cool situation, with renewed cold water application if symptoms reappear, is indicated.

In the sunny summer months, obviously more evident in hotter climates which includes much of America , canine 'hot spots' are not uncommon. A local irritation, or a flea, perhaps, encourages the dog to scratch, resulting in a reddened patch of skin which becomes moist. The surrounding hair also appears slightly damp. If not attended to promptly, these 'hot spots' have the propensity to develop into a serious skin condition. The American guide dog schools have this problem well under control, and both trainers and owners groom and inspect the dog diligently at least once daily so that early detection and subsequent treatment with appropriate veterinary applications is effected. Also, the source of scratching, if an external parasite, must be eliminated. In Britain, 'hot spots' are rather a rarity, but nonetheless might be in evidence during exceptionally warm spells of weather.

Ticks and fleas are a nuisance to dogs in Great Britain, but even more so in the United States. Thorough and regular grooming and use of insecticides is the best way to eradicate these external parasites, and guide dog schools on both sides of the Atlantic are scrupulous in instructing and encouraging owners to maintain these methods of ridding the animal of fleas, ticks and lice as and when and if they appear. Repeated use of insecticides may be necessary since the flea lays its eggs close to the root of the hair in a warm part of the body, and, if left for 10 or 14 days, these eggs hatch and cause a fresh infestation of the dog.

The flea, acting as vector, is responsible for the spread of some canine internal parasites, in particular tapeworm, and it is therefore imperative that these pests be destroyed immediately upon detection. Since fleas and ticks may have dropped off the dog and be harboured in the animal's bedding, and indeed carpets, crevices and furniture within the house, the Americans bring into very effective use 'room foggers' which are a type of fumigatory product strong enough to kill off both adult fleas and larvae (as well as other insect pests) which may be hiding in the house.

Diarrhoea evidences itself from time to time in dogs in Britain and America. It is an indication rather than a specific disease; an indication that some other major or minor cause has brought about diarrhoea. A cause such as scavenging and eating undesirable or tainted food, a change in water or diet, a change of environment. Internal parasites, or a virus may bring about a more serious spell of diarrhoea. If the condition persists, the veterinarian will need to be consulted and a stool examination conducted, but not before a 24-hour starvation period has been tried, followed by a few days on a bland diet with an additive such as bran or a proprietary brand of diarrhoea curative.

A not uncommon intestinal parasite in some parts of the United States is giardia, which can infrequently infect humans, but more usually dogs, cats and other animals. Carriers, and subsequent cross-infection, may occur between animal and humans unless strict cleanliness and disinfection procedures are pursued. Giardiasis is caused by a microscopic protozoan parasite which invariably results in diarrhoea. The disease can be transmitted through ingestion of contaminated water or food. In spite of a wholesome and adequate diet, infection may result in loss of weight and persistent diarrhoea. Only by detecting the parasite through microscopic inspection of the suspected faeces can the presence of giardia be confirmed, and expedient treatment initiated.

*   *   *   *

Each morning when we rise we wash ourselves and comb and brush our hair before setting out on our daily tasks. In much the same way, the guide dog owner is encouraged to carry out a daily grooming routine with regard to his charge, so that the animal retains a clean, healthy coat, and presents a pleasing appearance, and so that any external parasites or concealed wounds might be uncovered.

To be effective, grooming must reach skin level so that all loose and matted hair might be removed, and so that dirt is expelled, and any cutaneous infection such as eczema or mange is revealed, so that it can be effectively treated in the early stages. Also, blood circulation is stimulated by the vigorous action of the grooming brush, which should be of strong, but not excessively firm, bristle. For larger dogs, such as are guides, a horse dandy-brush is ideal, together with a durable metal comb. First, the coat, all over, from head to toe, and obviously exercising care around vulnerable areas such as the eyes and ears, is combed through. Then the coat is combed and brushed against the lie of the hair. Further combing follows, this time with the lie of the coat, concluding with a brief but intensive spell of brushing. Needless to say, grooming is best undertaken out-of-doors, so that the many stray hairs will waft away harmlessly with the wind.

If the dog is dirty or smelly, it can be bathed. Warm water, soap and a course towel are all that is needed. Dowse the dog amply, lather all over with brisk hand application, thoroughly rinse the animal, let it enjoy a good shake and then vigorously towel, concluding by combing the coat. It will still take a little while for the dog to completely dry out, preferably in the rays of the sun, or the warmth of the fireside.

Guide dogs are protected from those lethal canine diseases of hard pad, distemper, hepatitis, leptospira and parvovirus by vaccination at an early age. At two or three yearly intervals booster inoculations may be needed. The veterinarian will advise in this respect. In the United States, guide dogs are also inoculated against rabies, with a booster vaccination every three years.

Another canine complaint endemic to the United States, and nonexistent in Britain (thanks to its temperate climate) is heartworm (filariasis). These internal parasites, when adult, infest the heart and surrounding blood vessels, with the result that the infected dog has a reduced capacity for exercise, breathes laboriously, and is generally debilitated.

Adult heartworms are three to 15 inches long, and an eighth of an inch in diameter; by blocking the blood vessels of the heart and surrounding area circulation is affected to the extent that heart failure occurs in the heavily infested dog.

The mature heartworm produces microscopic larvae, microfilaria, which circulate throughout the body as they are carried along in the bloodstream. Mosquitoes feeding on an infected animal ingest these microfilaria. After a short stage of development in the insect, the larvae are transmitted to another dog when it is visited and bitten by the infectious mosquito.

Where heartworm in the canine is diagnosed, veterinary treatment using a toxic chemical is deemed necessary, followed by drugs to rid the dog of microfilaria. By far the better course of action is to administer a preventive drug such as diethylcarbamazine citrate which, taken daily, assures protection. Guide dog schools in the United States adopt these daily safety measures against the heartworm menace.

The roundworm is a common internal parasite of the young dog, where it lives in the small intestine. Eggs are passed out in the faeces and if ingested by another dog the life-cycle begins again. Roundworm infection in puppies results in diarrhoea, vomiting, debility, dull coat, and a pot-bellied, thin appearance. Infestation can be eradicated by the drug piperazine, and puppies as young as two weeks can be treated.

Dogs going out to puppy-walkers will have been treated in this way, with a follow-up administration of drugs at regular intervals after initial dosage. In adult dogs the worm is inactive. In fact, it encysts and lies dormant in the body tissues, only becoming activated through hormonal changes in the pregnant bitch, when the larvae then penetrate the uterus to infect the developing puppies.

Fleas, lice, uncooked offal, can all harbour the initial larval stage of tapeworms, which are flat, segmented parasites, several feet long and living in the intestines of the dog, to the inner wall of which it tenaciously attaches itself with a combination of hooks and suckers borne by the head portion. The small, white segments, about the size of a grain of rice, contain hundreds of eggs and are carried out of the body in the faeces, or may be found occasionally in the hair around the canine anus. A single tapeworm will have little detrimental effect on an adult dog, but heavy infestation can result in weight loss, dull coat and poor appetite. Also, an infected animal is the source of further spread of the parasite. Reliable drugs are available to expel tapeworms. Indeed, there are now veterinary preparations available in a single dosage which will eradicate all internal parasites harboured in the canine gut. Even where worm infection cannot be confirmed, nothing is lost in treating the suspect adult dog. In fact, bi-annual worming regimes for guide dogs - all dogs - are to be recommended.

A wholesome diet; clean, fresh water; ample free exercise in a safe area; strict weight control; an active working routine; up-dated vaccination against disease; a daily grooming schedule; control of parasites, and veterinary check-ups at six-monthly intervals are the corner-stones which lead to canine health and longevity. Both in Britain and North America, as with similar organizations world-wide, the various training centres are deeply aware of the values of fundamental canine health care, and the students who pass through their hands are thus well advised in these vital matters, with the result that guide dogs returning home with their new owners are assured of a continuing disease and ailment free, and consequently happy, existence in their fresh surroundings.

───── *16* ─────

After-Care

Having discussed the importance of control by the guide dog owner over his charge if he wishes to maintain and increase high standards of canine performance, it might be imagined that expectations of the blind person's ability to effect this avenue of training are unduly high. This is not so. Without denying the fact that a great deal is expected of the student during training, the trainer would certainly not be unwise enough to set unattainable heights insofar as the blind person's capacity is concerned. Nevertheless, the significance of control over the dog is constantly stressed, and opportunities afforded during team training to put such corrective moves into practice. The trainer, observing the novice unit at work, and following discreetly yet closely at hand during these early stages, will cue the student as to when a source of canine distraction is to appear, and thus the blind person can administer correction at the opportune moment, to the dismay of the dog which might have been thinking that a change of hand would afford the occasion for a drop in concentration and the taking of libertine steps.

In those cases where the agency considers a novice unit to be needful of further help in these matters of control, as well as other spheres of guide dog activity, even after the duration of class training, it is not unknown, and it is of considerable worth, for the trainer to accompany the unit home and work with the pair in the local environment for a few days. This practice, which can be most beneficial to the raw and perhaps not quite so positive, or so capable, guide dog owner, is known as *immediate after-care.*

Deciding upon choice routes to reach particular destinations can be a problem to many guide dog owners, and matters such as this, with help from the trainer, can be sorted out on the spot. The shortest journey is not necessarily the best, and by reconnaissance of a proposed route, the trainer can indicate to the blind person the safest and easiest crossing points. To initiate a new route merits a good deal of control from the guide dog owner, since his charge - at first - will be unsure of the unfamiliar environment in which it finds itself. Here again, the presence of the trainer will be a stabilizing influence on both parties.

All manner of things might be dealt with during immediate after-care, from the simplest (e.g., introducing the new dog to other family members) to the more complicated (a difficult route, perhaps, involving busy crossings and tube train travel), but all of them worthy of the attention of a trainer where a new and inexperienced guide dog owner is lacking in confidence and, maybe, ability. The elderly and more incapacitated blind person will similarly derive benefit from immediate after-care.

Even where the polished and proficient performer is concerned after-care can be advantageous. Extremely capable guide dog owners can, like all of us, make mistakes, or traverse routes which, with forethought, could perhaps be made simpler and safer. Also, a short and intensive on-the-spot stint of refresher training, based primarily on a familiar route in the local environment, but with artificial obstacle and traffic work thrown in for good measure, does not do any harm to even the most efficient guide dog and its owner. For this reason, many guide dog training agencies indulge in *routine after-care*, whereby all units are visited on a regular, once a year basis.

In this way, as well as guide dog performance being monitored, canine health and welfare can also be checked. If the dog is too fat, the trainer will recommend appropriate action to be taken by the owner to cut down the animal's weight - less food and more exercise. Similarly, he will be advised to seek veterinary attention if the dog appears to be ailing for some reason or another, notwithstanding the obligatory six-monthly canine health check-ups.

Routine after-care provides an opportunity for replacement of worn-out guide dog accoutrements, for the trainer and blind person to perhaps renew old acquaintanceships, and for the latter to be kept informed of any changes in the philosophy of the agency that might have taken place during the previous year, and which could be of some relevance to the guide dog owner.

As well as being a format for the exchange of news, views and achievements, as a background to the more important viewing by the visiting trainer of the unit's work and capability during the stipulated 30 or 60 minute walk, when obstacle and traffic work is reinforced together with other areas which merit attention, routine after-care provides a platform for both trainer and owner to make future canine replacement plans in those cases where an older guide dog is concerned. The dog, for instance, might be approaching 10 years old, and both human parties will be asking themselves questions as to whether the animal is now beginning to slow down appreciably; are its responses sufficient to meet the demands of guiding; is its eyesight still sharp; are its joints becoming arthritic; is its general health good? On the basis of the answers to these questions, the need for a replacement dog will be discussed.

Should there be a waiting list of applicants for guide dogs on an agency's books, the returning blind person would not be affected by this, since guide dog owners needing replacement animals automatically take precedence and go to the head of the queue. Once a decision is made regarding the retirement of a guide dog, there is therefore only the minimum of lapse in time before the blind person attends for training with a new dog.

Most dogs have a working life of eight or nine years, so at the age of 10 or 11 retirement plans will be being made both by the agency, upon the prompting of the trainer carrying out routine after-care, and by the owner who himself will obviously be aware of declining ability and performance in the old dog. Nevertheless, dogs are very much individuals as far as ageing is concerned, and a number of older animals still retain their capability and vitality and go on working to a more advanced age. Conversely, others are retired in their younger years.

A decision must also be taken by the guide dog owner as to what to do with the old dog when it is retired. Will he keep it when he is assigned a replacement guide dog? Two dogs in a household, especially where one is old and perhaps incapacitated and therefore needs extra attention, can be quite a handful, yet many blind persons do keep the old dog in its twilight years. This is more often the case where a family is concerned. A blind person living on his own might face difficulties in looking after two dogs, especially if he is out at work all day. In this case he may perforce keep only the replacement dog. When this happens, the agency finds a retirement home for the old dog, since there are those people who are kind enough to take an aged animal into their house and look after it until its days are ended.

It is rare but not unknown for guide dogs to be withdrawn for shoddy work, whether from the canine angle or the human angle, or a combination of both. Dogs which have become so inhibited that their responses to the various stimuli offered them are non-existent, and where the owner has been unable, or unwilling, or indeed where it has proved impossible, to reinforce these missing responses with success. Persistent over-shooting of kerbs, for instance; a non-central position on the pavement to the extent that the animal is either almost walking in the gutter or scraping along the sides of garden walls; failure to respond to traffic or obstacles; inadequate right shoulder work. These, and other examples of faded conditioning may mean that a guide dog is withdrawn, and the blind person, if still considered suitable by the agency (particularly where it is plain that the fault lies with the dog, or in the manner of training the two together) and if he is still interested, after what might have been a traumatic experience, in returning for training, he will be matched with another more suitable dog.

The gradual growth of previously dormant temperamental faults may indicate that a guide dog should be withdrawn. Protective aggression or pure aggression: traffic suspicion; poor concentration; acute dog distraction, or cat or general distraction, for example. Or embarrassing social behaviour, or a health problem, can account for early withdrawal of a guide dog. Again, an alternative animal will most probably be offered in these cases of guide dog failure.

Routine after-care offers the opportunity for crass faults such as described to be discovered. It may be that the problem, if disclosed at an early stage, can, with the aid of the trainer, be overcome on the spot. Failing this, a short refresher course, perhaps at the training centre, can help. The examples of poor social behaviour, protective aggression and dog distraction provide instances where therapy under the guidance or advice of a trainer may make recovery possible.

It is more often in the pursuit of *emergency after-care,* however, that radical faults have to be dealt with as far as the guide dog unit is concerned. The guide dog owner always maintains contact with the agency, so that if a fault crops up he can write or phone and, at the earliest, a trainer will travel to see him and deal with the problem at first hand. Usually, it is the novice guide dog units which profess trouble, and often the problem is found to be rather magnified and the stabilizing hand of the trainer puts matters right.

In more serious instances, however, refresher courses, or, at worst, withdrawal can be indicated, often because of one, or a combination of some of the temperamental or failed training faults as outlined previously. Bearing in mind the great number of guide dog units which are trained each year, and the grand total of working partnerships which ensue, withdrawals for defective work are a comparative rarity.

17

FUTURE PROSPECTS

With the guide dog unit working alone, at home, those first few days of solo efforts will bring some measure of happiness and not a little heartache. As the weeks go by, and the team gradually co-ordinates, for many guide dog owners it becomes plain sailing and silly mistakes, both human and canine, made previously become a thing of the past. For most handlers, the hard work initially expended is put behind them, and relaxation and confidence are the keywords in their new-found mobility with their keen and efficacious guide dogs.

But regrettably there are those few guide dog owners for whom things don't seem to work out as well as they would have wished. Even during training the student might have been concerned at his lack of 'oneness' with his new dog, and felt inwardly that "This isn't the dog for me". But the reassuring remarks of the trainer, and his reiterations that all would be well once the unit had 'gelled' after a few month's work at home, so long as the blind person puts into practice that which was being preached at the training centre, would help to dispel any fears.

Of course, it is true that a guide dog unit, to be efficient, must work as a closely knit team, and the dog, to derive quality performance from it as a guide, must be constantly kept up to scratch by the handler through a balanced mixture of praise and chastisement as befits the animal's behaviour at a given time.

We are all well aware of the fact that (as to all animals, including *homo sapiens*) praise for good behaviour, and punishment for recalcitrance usually encourages the dog, on future occasions, to perform the former to the exclusion of the latter. Imagine the consequences if these two important conditions of training were reversed. Happily, it is seldom that a guide dog user, difficult though differentiation might be, makes the mistake of praising the dog when it is behaving badly (for instance, saying "Good dog" whilst the animal is sniffing a lamp post) or chastises the dog when it is doing well (saying "Bad dog" as the canine cleverly negotiates an obstacle). To the credit of the guide dog owner's discriminatory powers, such events are rare.

More common, however, are the following two phenomena: not praising the dog *enough* at *precisely* the time it is doing a good deed, and not *admonishing the dog enough* at *precisely the moment* it is behaving badly. The feeling expressed in the voice of the guide dog owner should be sufficient to impart to the dog the note of pleasure or displeasure which it is hoped to convey.

On occasion, it may be that the verbal chastisement will be accompanied by physical correction. Once the dog stops its bad behaviour and reverts to good conduct, punishment ceases and is replaced by praise for so doing. To effect good management of the dog, therefore, ideally the guide dog user should apply, when appropriate, these two conditions of trained behaviour, praise (positive reinforcement) and punishment (negative reinforcement), in such a way as to be responded to by the dog.

Similarly, the dog in the handler's care should be of such a sensitivity and temperament that it is *receptive* to his wishes. In other words, it would be unwise to allocate a dog to a blind person which is beyond the capacity of that person to manage.

One might imagine that all one needs to do is to supply a guide dog (the mobility tool) to a blind person and the task of safe, independent travel will henceforth prove of no problem to the recipient of the dog. But even after skilled and intensive training, which is the vital and obligatory precursor to guide dog ownership, if it is found that things seem to go wrong, with the animal not living up to expectations, and the user complaining about the dog's shortcomings, do we then claim that only "a bad workman quarrels with his tools"?

True you can't very well blame the fishing rod if you can't catch any fish, but if the rod is so ill-constructed that it constantly comes apart at badly fitting joints, or the necessary pliability isn't present to give a good cast, or the line snags and frays on poorly designed and fitted eyelets, then there might be every justification in pointing the finger of suspicion at the rod for lack of luck during fishing expeditions.

Dare we draw a parallel here with the guide dog? It would be wrong to cast aspersions on the animal when a good dog is being mishandled by an incompetent owner. But it would be just as wrong to blame the handler when the pair were mis-matched in the first place, or the dog has faults (suspicion, aggression, distraction, poor social behaviour, excessive speed impossible to control) which no amount of expert handling could possibly correct. It would be then that the guide dog owner would have a legitimate grouse.

We are of course raising here philosophical questions. If all guide dogs allocated are of top quality material, and trained to the peak of perfection, one might postulate that all guide dog units subsequently will display high standards of performance. But this is precluded by the divergent dynamics involved in human and canine interaction, coupled with the fact that all guide dogs will not (and cannot, just like their human partners) be of top quality material (because top quality is an abstract and relative term which cannot accurately be defined or attained).

Similarly with 'peak of perfection'. As far as training is concerned, where is the peak? Once upon a time it was thought that the four-minute mile was the height of achievement in athletics. But where will it end? The peak of perfection in guide dog training, which, like so many other peaks, is unattainable, is also held back in the valiant but vain attempts to reach it by the varying limitations of the trainer, and then the blind handler. That is to say, a good quality dog will achieve a standard nearer the peak than a poorer quality dog, and a capable trainer will set standards for that dog (and indeed reach such standards) than will a less-capable or less knowledgeable or less-conscientious trainer or handler.

One might equate guide dog training (and for that matter all forms of mobility training) with an educational process, which indeed it is. If the peak of perfection could be reached for *everyone* within the educational system, then one might assume that everyone would end up as a university graduate. But, as we all know, the initial intellect and temperament and learning capacity of the student holds much sway during the educational process, as does the intellect and teaching capacity and capability of the teacher concerned. Coupled with this are the environmental factors (number of pupils in class, catchment area, physical surroundings). So it is that we don't all graduate at a university, and so it is that, for parallel reasons, all guide dog units don't perform as one might hope they would.

It is important for the guide dog user to understand that success with his new mobility aid does not come overnight. There is a lot of effort to be expended (as has been demonstrated to him during training) and trials and tribulations to contend with before, whether in a matter of weeks or months, the unit begins to work as one and reap the rewards of joint human and canine labours by way of the former's enhanced and safer mobility in an atmosphere free of stress. With a well-matched team expertly trained together, such a satisfactory situation should not take too long to evolve.

Since most guide dog units prove to be a good match, success subsequently follows. On odd occasions, however, matters may not seem quite right, and indefinable (sometimes definable) feelings of doubt and disenchantment persist with his dog and its performance perhaps with increasing consciousness in the mind of the blind person.

These feelings might be justified, and should be respected by the trainer and the agency concerned. At the same time the guide dog owner must not allow unsubstantiated feelings to overshadow reality. He should be aware of particular canine potential which might display itself in the future rather than the immediate present. Where compelling doubts persist however - doubts which may evidence themselves in practice - it would be unwise to continue with this team of man and dog. As in residential training, so it is in the domiciliary setting. Where it is blatantly obvious in the observed performance over a period of time that the match is unsatisfactory, one should have no hesitation in withdrawing the dog. There is a limit to the bounds of perseverance. Also it is grossly unfair to make excessive demands of the blind person.

Every person is a separate and unique individual, and the solution to esoteric mobility needs is similarly separate and unique. Therefore a blanket approach to training guide dog units, although acceptable in the earlier and more fundamental aspects, usually is dispensed with as more complex training practicalities are dealt with. This is why, at the more involved stages of training, the trainer tailors the work to suit the capabilities and requirements of the individual student. This is why also the student should be guided competently and honestly as to future mobility prospects with his guide dog by his trainer, who has (or should have) the necessary expertise to determine the long term outlook for the unit, which must be sanguine, otherwise the whole exercise is futile and a colossal waste of time. A rosy outlook for the team has its roots in an initial propitious match of man and dog as decided by the trainer.

──── *18* ────

ALTERNATIVE MOBILITY AIDS

The mobility of blind persons increasingly attracts the attention not only of the consumer but of various relevant agencies and social work departments of many local authorities. The upsurge of interest has been especially marked since the introduction, from the United States, of travel techniques for the blind using the long cane method and involving orientation (use of sensory perception to establish relationship to, and knowledge of, one's surroundings) and mobility (movement from one point to another or, as Dr Leslie Kay more accurately defines it, "those skills and knowledge which enable one to walk unobtrusively among one's fellow men"). So much so that a number of local authorities and voluntary organisations and schools employ mobility instructors.

Loss of mobility is perhaps the most profound physical consequence of blindness, and this in itself might bring about allied emotional inconsonance which may be difficult to alleviate in the visually handicapped person. Stemming from the research, immediately after the last war, of Dr Richard E. Hoover of the Veterans Administration Hospital in Illinois, USA, interest in the furtherance of mobility for the blind has spread rapidly. In his efforts to get war blinded soldiers mobile again, it was Hoover who devised the long cane technique of travel which is now being used by an ever-increasing number of visually impaired people.

But orientation and mobility training involves more than simply travelling alone on a short journey along the pavement. It embraces a whole range of features besides. Orientation training is bent on capturing the widest possible use of senses other than sight which will assist a blind person to gain a fuller knowledge of his surroundings, and consequently render his mobility that much better. Memory, hearing, touch, positional sense, smell, ability to take bearings and assess direction are all exercised, trained and developed to the full so that maximum benefit towards successful mobility is thus derived.

The technique of using the long cane is basically one in which the stick is manipulated to evolve a passage for the blind pedestrian, and provide protection at the same time. The long cane is held in the right hand in the mid-body position from which point it is pivoted by dextrous movement of the wrist, and the artefact is directed, at an angle of 45 degrees, so that the tip explores the ground immediately in front and a pace ahead of where the pedestrian is about to tread. That is, the right foot moves forward to the previous cleared position as the cane is swung across the width of the body, tip at ground level, to momentarily but thoroughly investigate the spot where the next step will be placed with the left foot. And so the movements of the cane are alternated in an arc from side to side as each successive stride is taken.

Since the strokes of the cane are synchronised with the steps there is an even and continuous flow of movement forward by the pedestrian. If the cane point reports an obstruction or a drop or rise in the terrain, the traveller is alerted to avoid the danger or come to a stop. Though the use of the aid provides protection for the body from the waist down, and forewarns the user to ground level variations and obstacles which are rooted to the pavement, such as posts and barriers, defence of chest and head from overhangs is unfortunately precluded. The long cane is made of a light, durable alloy, either rigid or collapsible, and the length is dependent upon the individual's height, posture and pace width.

Whilst the long cane technique might be a comparatively new means of travel, the time-honoured modes of guide dog and white stick remain constant. The long cane is but one facet of blind mobility to take its place along the more tested types, and it is a welcome one. For not only is it advantageous to have a wider range of choices in mobility tools open to the blind, it is also useful in that it stimulates publicity detailing the problems of mobility generally. And the consumer is additionally made more aware of the variety of options open to him when deciding on a mobility aid. It is probably true to say that the advent of the long cane, since it focused so finely on the benefits of efficient and safe travel for the blind, evoked an even higher demand for guide dogs than hitherto.

Not surprisingly, a number of notions deployed in guide dog mobility have rubbed off on long cane travel, more especially when dealing with the environment: use of the mid-pavement position when walking, for instance, as well as some aspects of kerb drill and dealing with traffic, not to mention self alignment with the flow of vehicles on the road alongside which the blind person is making his way whilst remaining central on the sidewalk, which helps to determine direction and situation.

The crux of the mobility matter is obviously the blind person himself. To get around independently, and to employ a mobility aid towards maximum benefit, whether guide dog, long cane or anything else, a blind person must be aware of the nature of the environment about him and of the problems it might present: he should be aware of his location in that environment; and the direction in which he is travelling; he should preferably be aware of any potential hazards that might lie ahead; and he should be resourceful enough to surmount any difficulties which crop up - a resource, indeed, that extends to the solicitation of sighted help if the situation warrants it. This expediency is a valuable way of overcoming an impasse.

Since over 85 per cent of environmental and external information is gained visually, the uncertainties facing the blind are considerable. Because of this the practice of orientation and mobility places much stress on the constructive use of the remaining senses - senses, incidentally, which are no better than a sighted persons, but become more discriminatory through necessity and use. Hearing and touch are the two mainstays for a totally blind person, the development and discerptibility of which can add much to environmental perception and mobility.

Auditory clues can provide useful information to a blind person in a variety of ways, giving hints, for instance, as to the flow and density of traffic; the location of a bus shelter; the position of a lift or escalator; the site of a school or other buildings. Similar examples abound, where a discrete sense of hearing is invaluable. Touch is obviously vital for braille reading (although only five per cent of the total blind population can use this medium), but also in the identification of objects and landmarks, and indeed in perceiving any change in terrain which might provide information as to location or warning of hidden danger, such as the upturned earth of a pavement being repaired, or cables and gravel littering the pathway.

Less helpful in orientation and mobility, but nevertheless useful, are the senses of smell (to help locate a pub, fish and chip shop, baker's, butcher's, florist's, etc.) and taste, the latter being mainly for internal information. Coupled with all this, a well-developed spatial awareness is always an invaluable asset to the blind person wishing to further his mobility. It may mean, for instance, that he has no need to count his footsteps to a particular location, whether indoors or outdoors, or grope for a light switch, a cupboard door, a long cane in the corner or a guide dog harness on a coat hook.

Training in long cane mobility is usually domiciliary, although the facility is available at most rehabilitation centres for the blind, and takes place over varied periods of time, dependent upon age, ability and aptitude, and instruction ceases at differing levels and stages to suit particular individuals. Besides tuition in the actual manipulation of the long cane in such a way as to afford maximum protection and information to the user, also to be fostered and encouraged is the whole range of sensory skills which will further enhance mobility. Additionally involved are the techniques of moving about indoors, either without a cane or employing it in a modified manner; the 'daily living skills' that the seeing take so much for granted; methods of movement when escorted by a sighted person; the location of objects and landmarks; the localisation and discrimination of sound in order to reach a destination; shopping; bus and train travel; ascending and descending stairs; entering and leaving cars; familiarisation cues in unfamiliar buildings: these and more are entailed in training a blind person to become a safer and more self-reliant traveller. Indeed, the progression towards that goal is in many ways parallel to the technique of travel with a guide dog. Guide dog owners, too, rely a great deal on the discerning deployment of different senses, but much is left, as it should be, to the 'seeing-eye' and the sagacity of the canine as far as safe mobility is concerned.

Age for age, and generally speaking, the guide dog owner progresses more rapidly and with less stress than users of other mobility aids; he travels with little need to concentrate on the matter in hand, and consequently looks more self-assured; and he is not so obvious as a blind pedestrian because, mostly, he is unobtrusive, and aesthetically more pleasing to the onlooker.

On the other hand a long cane offers apprehensible and entirely independent travel with a sense of self-accomplishment at the successful end to a journey. In addition, it does not need to be fed and watered, housed, groomed and exercised; it does not fall sick at awkward times, or spread hairs or mud on rugs or Sunday-best clothes; nor does it have a comparatively short life. Yet nor does it give happy companionship, the emotional satisfaction brought about in caring for a dependent animal, and a mutual trust that evokes confidence in spheres wider than that of pure mobility.

In the eyes of the general public efficient blind travel is epitomised by the guide dog. But a blind person is interested only in the mobility aid that happens to suit him best. For some, a guide dog will be the answer, for others, it will be the long cane that proves most beneficial. Still others will be content (or must needs be content) with a white stick, or indeed no mobility device whatsoever. And let it be said that self-help can still be the best mobility aid of all - or, at least, the best preparation for future training with a long cane or guide dog.

Although even the simplest tasks can be less problematical with professional guidance, successful mobility is initiated and built upon through individual effort. To gather self-confidence and awareness of the environment a blind person should get out and about and explore his neighbourhood - firstly, perhaps with a sighted escort, but secondly, and carefully, alone. And if the prospective guide dog user can also find prior training in the long cane technique, then all to the good - two strings to the bow are better than one!

The lack of protection afforded the user to the upper part of the body places some limitation on the value of the long cane. Electronic attachments to the artefact can help counteract this to a certain extent, and research in this direction has led to the development of the laser cane, which looks like and is used in the same way as a long cane.

The laser cane houses an electronic device, powered by battery, which emits three narrow beams of invisible infra-red light. The *straight ahead beam* projects forward, about one metre from and parallel with ground level, and picks up objects within a range of four metres. The reflected beam warns the user both tactually, by vibrating pins in the handle of the cane, and audibly, by a low pitched buzz, to the presence of solid objects immediately ahead. An *angled upward beam* forewarns the user, via higher pitched sound emission, of head height obstacles, whilst an *angled downward beam* gives out a distinctive intermittent noise pattern if steps, down-kerbs and holes in the ground lie directly ahead.

Whilst the laser cane is gainful in forewarning the user of hindrance and dangers which bestrew his path, and of thus protecting him somewhat from harm, as with all mechanical mobility devices it places severe restriction on brisk and stress-free pedestrian travel, whereas a good guide dog will be a balancing factor in these two important directions, yet still maintaining safety and independence.

The laser cane is helpful for a blind person who has the additional handicap of deafness since it is a mobility aid which imparts information tactually (through the vibrating pins inserted in the handle) as well as audibly. Of use to a visually handicapped person who is confined to a wheelchair, and thus unable to use a cane in the conventional sense, is the Russell pathsounder. This device is suspended on a neck strap on the chest, and emits ultrasound of such high frequency that it is unable to be detected by the human ear. However, should the beam meet up with a solid object ahead, the sound is electronically reorganised and becomes audible as it is reflected back to the pathsounder; the nearer the obstacle, the higher pitched is the tone emitted. To help the deaf-blind, tactile vibrators are fitted to the neck strap. There is also a head-mounted model of the pathsounder, so that the way ahead can be monitored simply by moving the head to left or right. The device is useful for finding openings - if doors happen to remain unclosed, that is – since lack of noise between a left and right beam from the pathsounder obviously indicates a space. For an incapacitated blind person in a wheelchair, the Russell pathsounder can impart mobility information which will be at least of a little value.

Operating on the same principle as the pathsounder by way of reflected ultrasound, but this time converted purely tactually rather than audibly, is the Mowat sensor, which is a hand-held torch-like device. It may be scanned from side to side so that the ultrasound beam covers an arc in front of the user, and should the ray strike a solid object it is bounced back to the sensor where it is converted into electrical impulses which causes the device to vibrate in the hand. The quicker the impulses, the nearer the object. A similar device is the Nottingham obstacle detector (NOD) which, rather than vibrations to indicate proximity of objects, makes use of a rather pleasing musical scale. The sensor and the detector are useful in locating specific points such as post boxes, telephone kiosks, bus stops, pedestrian crossings, railings, openings and the like. In this respect, the sensor and detector are not really mobility aids, but, carried in the pocket or handbag of a long cane user or guide dog owner they may be produced to ascertain proximity of a bus stop or similar landmark which is sought. The guide dog, however, with practice and familiarity should resort promptly, and close to, the likes of a bus stop upon a word of command from the owner as the destination is being neared. At times, in fact, a little too close to the stop, somewhat (perhaps) to the embarrassment of the guide dog user when his charge takes him to the head of a long queue, rather than the end of it!

Vision is the most valuable mobility aid of all. Electronic travel devices such as those we have discussed are perfunctory substitutes for eyesight, and also call for some tuition, and much skill and interpretation on the part of the user if he wishes to derive benefit from their employment. Indeed, the commonest aid of all is still that old stand-by, the stout, white stick. This is so because, with the vast majority of blind people being old and consequently a little feeble, the two major requirements of a mobility aid in this respect are that they supply physical support to the user, and indicate to other members of the public that he is blind, and may therefore need some help and consideration. The white stick is generally not used as a guiding aid, although it does indeed act as a buffer and can impart some rudimentary information as to what lies immediately ahead. A white stick with broad, red bands around it indicates that the user is deaf as well as blind.

Often enough, a person with a white stick, and indeed other mobility aids including guide dogs, will make use of a sighted escort to expedite journeys or help in awkward situations. Acting the part of sighted guide for a blind person calls for some measure of awareness and skill from both escort and escorted. It is important, firstly, that the blind person takes his escort's arm and not the other way about.

A sighted person might make the mistake of man-handling a blind person in an attempt to guide him. It is far simpler, and much more comfortable and efficacious for the blind person to take the arm of the escort, but the sighted guide should first of all enquire as to whether or not assistance is required. It is not unknown for a bewildered blind person to be frog-marched by a well-meaning but misguided sighted individual over a road he does not want to cross. Sometimes, indeed, to be abandoned in the middle of the road, or, having reached the up-kerb to be left there without further enquiry as to which direction he now wishes to take.

The blind person can link arms with his escort, or lightly grip the upper limb above the elbow, either on the left or right, but if a guide dog owner with his charge, the sighted individual will be always on the right. At all times, a guide dog, whether in harness or on the lead, remains on the left. If a guide dog owner is being escorted by a sighted person, and his dog is wearing harness, the handle is allowed to rest on the animal's back whilst the lead is retained in the left hand. When the pedestrian journey envisaged by the guide dog owner and his sighted escort is a lengthy one, the harness should not be worn.

By taking the escort's arm just above the elbow, the blind person travels half a pace behind his sighted guide, and a confident duo may now walk at their ease where they will. If a narrow space or doorway is encountered, the escort puts his guiding arm behind him, whilst the blind person straightens his own connecting arm to its fullest extent and walks behind the sighted individual in single file, to go through the gap without losing contact.

Chancing upon changes in level, kerbs, steps up or down, and other eventualities, the sighted guide momentarily stops and verbally and descriptively intimates the nature of the hindrance. "One step down", "A flight of steps up", "A steep ramp down", and thus the blind person is acquainted with what lies ahead.

When going through a doorway, it is useful for the blind person to be on the hinged side of the door, so that the two will not be in a state of disarray as they try to open and close it behind them. To change sides so that the escort is furthest away from the hinges, the blind person goes behind his guide, still maintaining contact, and takes the other arm of the sighted individual. By so doing, smooth progression is facilitated, since, as the escort opens the door, the blind person slides his arm down that of his guide to take the handle, and in fact keeps the door open for both himself and the sighted individual as they proceed through the doorway. In this way, the blind person is also able to close the door behind him, without his sighted escort having to tie himself in knots endeavouring to do so, which would be the case if he were on the wrong side of the individual he is guiding.

If the blind person has a guide dog with him whilst making use of an escort, he can, for this brief interval of time when going through the doorway, switch the dog to his right. However, although a little more inconvenience might be suffered in opening and closing the door, it will be just as well to keep the dog on the left. Certainly, when the blind person is working his dog in harness, and the door is to be opened and closed to allow passage, the animal remains on the left. The dog approaches close to the doorway and waits for the handler to open the door, stepping back with the owner as he does so (if the door opens outward). Dependent upon which way the door opens, the blind person may find it more convenient to momentarily drop the handle on the dog's back and just retain the lead as the doorway is negotiated. Once through the space, and having closed the door, the handle is picked up again and man and dog resume their journey. The blind person must take care not to trap the dog's tail whilst closing doors behind him. If revolving doors need to be negotiated, trapped tails and toes should be guarded against, and when going through these doors the lead only should be retained.

Because of the differing nature of doorways, door negotiation is often a matter of modification to suit the circumstances. A minority of dogs are astute enough to approach close to a shut door and 'point' with their noses to the handle. Taking a tactile line from nose to handle helps the blind person to quickly find the opening catch. But even without this canine indication, most door handles, being situated more or less universally in the same place, are simple to detect.

A well-trained and experienced guide dog will invariably find a vacant chair on command when entering a room with its owner. Usually, it approaches to the front of the chalr. However, when a blind person is making use of a sighted escort and is being assisted to a chair, he should be shown to the back of the seat. All the escort need do is place the blind person's hand on the top of the back of the chair, and leave the rest to him. The blind person then himself goes to the front of the chair, feels the seat to determine height and check that it is empty, and takes his sitting position. A very simple and trouble-free operation which would be made most awkward and embarrassing if the blind person were to be pushed and manoeuvred manually into the seat as, regrettably, often happens if the escort is unaware of sighted guide procedure.

Getting into a car the system is again very much simplified through the expedience of leaving the blind person to manage for himself, with only the minimum of indication. All the escort need do is show the blind person the car door catch, by the latter sliding his hand down the former's guiding arm until it reaches the handle which is being grasped by the sighted individual. The escort's hand is then withdrawn, and the blind person, unaided, opens the car door, and, holding the top of the open doorway so that he doesn't bang his head as well as to afford support, takes his seat. If he has a guide dog with him, which will be on the lead only, it will be told to stay while its owner gets into the car, and is then called inside to sit at his feet in front of him.

The blind person does not close the door of the vehicle after him without first forewarning others that he is about to do so, in order to avoid trapped fingers. And then when leaving the car, he should first ask the driver if it is safe to open the door, in case there are obstructions or pedestrians passing by outside. Should the blind person have a guide dog with him, in this instance the animal can disembark first.

When meeting a blind person, identify yourself, and do let him know it is he you are addressing, otherwise he might think you are talking to someone else. Speak to a blind person normally; they are not deaf as well. And speak directly to him, and not through a third party, almost as if insinuating he is unable to think for himself, or hold a sensible conversation. And do not avoid words like "look or "see". They are part of the English language, and as such are used in conversation by the blind just as much as the sighted.

If you are hosting a blind visitor, show him around his room and indicate where the furniture is, also any potential head-height hazards. Let him know where the bathroom is. Don't leave doors half open, or change furniture around without telling him, or have things lying around the floor. When offering a cigarette, mention if it is filter-tipped, and provide an ashtray. At the table, tell your blind visitor what is in his dish. By imagining the plate as a clock face, the precise position of particular portions of food can be imparted. Ask if he would like his food cutting up, especially meat, although most blind people manage very well without such help.

Be especially careful when giving directions to a blind person. Do not make vague references to landmarks which he will be unable to identify. When leaving a blind person, tell him you are going, otherwise he might continue conversing to thin air. If boarding a bus, or going up or down stairs, it is helpful to gently place the blind person's hand on the support rail. And if you're in a cafe enjoying coffee with him, don't fill the cup too full thus making it difficult to drink without swilling some of the contents over the side.

Don't whisper to others in a blind person's presence - or anybody's presence for that matter. Avoid expressions of incredulity and praise at the many everyday tasks a blind person is well able to do after a little practice. Do not be flippant with idle remarks about the compensations that blindness brings. There are none. A blind person functions as an intelligent and self-sufficient individual mainly through the spirit of his own endeavour.

Epilogue

Although, in the main, the pattern of guide dog training both in Britain and the United States is much the same, there are one or two important differences upon which one might ponder as to wisdom when a particular technique is seen in practice. Length of training, for instance, which, in both countries generally involves two intensive walks daily for each individual dog per five day week. But in Britain the dog is trained over a period of at least five months, whereas in the States three months is the accepted length of time spent in the hands of the trainer before the dog is allocated to the blind person. Once this training is completed, in both Britain and the USA blind person and guide dog are trained together in two to four weeks. It should be mentioned that the British trainer deals with four blind students and their dogs during this residential course of human-canine team training, whilst his American counterpart handles six, or sometimes eight, such teams.

The British system involving a five-month span of training is more sophisticated than the American model. It is possibly also less labour intensive. In other words, more training staff are involved in perfecting the finished product. Most guide dogs in Britain are reared in the homes of people who are kind enough to keep, socialize and give elementary training to the puppies which are farmed out to them by the agency until, when mature, between 12 and 15 months old, they return to the training centre for advanced training.

These puppy-walkers provide an admirable and indispensible service for the agency and an overwhelming number of guide dogs emanate from this source. Similar schemes operate just as successfully in the USA. A small minority of dogs on both sides of the Atlantic originate from owners who offer adult dogs, up to the age of 30 months, and who, for one reason or another, cannot or do not want to keep their pets. The percentage of such animals accepted for training is, however, considerably less than puppy-walked dogs.

When prospective guide dogs arrive at the British training centre at conclusion of puppy-walking, they spend a couple of weeks in isolation kennels (to ascertain health and prevent possible infection) before undergoing a three-week testing period to measure temperamental suitability before acceptance. The dogs must be friendly, bold, biddable, and not be nervous or frightened by any feature of our modern environment. They must show a willingness to work, and be of good concentration. The same procedures and standards apply in the United States, but the commencement of training sees some differences emerge. Breeds of dogs used, too, are much the same. But breed is relatively unimportant; temperament, size and type are the more significant factors in guide dog acceptance, the majority of which will be bitches which will be spayed before training is concluded. However, many guide dogs are castrated males and, now that their worth is being proved, this percentage is on the increase.

In Britain, each GDBA training centre has a Dog Supply Unit (DSU), sometimes referred to as the Early Training Unit (ETU). The American schools do not. The assistant trainers in the ETU handle the budding guide dogs for the first two months of their five-month stint, during which the dogs are encouraged to walk with hindquarters at the left side of the trainer and going slightly ahead so that there is tautness, without excessive pulling, on the lead. The dogs must proceed in a straight line (deviating only for obstacles and other pedestrians) in the centre of the pavement and across intersecting roads. Within a short space of time the dogs are introduced to the harness and handle, the guiding link between man and dog. They are trained to sit at the down-kerb, and to respond to the directional commands of back, left and right, as well as the command "Forward" to move off. If distracted at any time, the dogs are corrected for such misdemeanours. Now the animals transfer from the ETU for advanced training at the hands of guide dog instructors who, whilst maintaining previous training, introduce obstacle work (the dog must leave the pavement to go round an obstruction which blocks the path, as well as overhangs which might be too low for a blind person to go under) and traffic work, where the dog learns to ignore the command "Forward" if moving vehicles are in dangerous proximity, and the dogs also learn to work safely in shops, restaurants, offices, railway stations, steps, lifts and public transport as well as differing pavement and road conditions from very quiet country lanes to the busiest of urban conditions, and all the varied street junctions that these offer.

Five months or so having elapsed, the trained guide dog is now ready for allocation to the blind student. In the States, however, all the afore-mentioned training, including that covered by the ETU, is completed by the guide dog instructor, without the intervention of an assistant trainer, in the space of three or, at the most, four months. Each of the centres in the States is separately and independently administered, whereas in Britain the GDBA collectively controls, from its headquarters in Hillfields, Burghfield Common, Reading, Berkshire, the training centres at Exeter, Bolton, Forfar, Wokingham, Middlesbrough, Leamington, Belfast and Woodford. The Mobility Aid and Guide Dog Alliance (MAGDA) is at Newcastle upon Tyne and Carlisle. The GDBA also has ancillary training units based in Cardiff, Maidstone, Glasgow and Nottingham.

The British dog having undertaken five month's training, and the American guide dog three months, the invidious question now asked will inevitably be: which is the better product? The answer, if such it could be called, is that it all depends on the quality of the particular dog to start with, the quality of the training it receives, and the quality of the blind person to whom it is ultimately allocated. In other words, a good dog turned out at the hands of a good trainer and subsequently assigned to a capable blind person will provide a first-rate guide dog team. To elaborate further, no two dogs are the same, no two trainers are the same, and no two blind people are the same, thus the quality of the finished product, whether trained over a period of three or five months, is bound to vary. What must be adhered to, as both the British and American schools do, is a minimum standard consistent with the requirements of capability, safety and appearance.

The vetting process of applicants for guide dogs is much the same in Britain and the United States. Each applicant is personally interviewed to test suitability for guide dog ownership, and only those who do not meet the moderate and flexible level of acceptance will be refused training with a guide dog. On paper, the guide dog and blind person are matched together to suit each other physically and, to some degree, what might loosely be termed as psychologically. Matching the two together will be confirmed, or altered, during the first three days after the blind person has arrived for his residential training, when the trainer can better assess at closer range the capabilities and attributes, or otherwise, of each particular blind person when he is considered against the dog thought best suited to him. Not all of these students will be training with their first dog; in fact, most of them will have had guide dogs before, which have now died or retired, and therefore they have arrived for instruction with a new dog.

Whilst residential training continues apace, attracting increasing attention also is domiciliary training, especially with regard to experienced guide dog owners who need replacement animals. Although limitations of professional manpower may restrict this activity, where it has been undertaken in the past, success is invariably the outcome.

Another important difference observed in America when compared to techniques in Britain is the stop at the kerb. In the States, guide dogs stop and stand at the down-kerb; in Britain, mostly, they sit. The American dogs stop at the up-kerb, which perhaps, but for the elderly person, is an unimportant practice. In fact, with reference to kerb drill, it seems that a combination of the two nations' strategies would be a sound proposition; that is, to stop and stand at the down-kerb to await the command "Forward", and not to stop at the up-kerb, but to proceed directly onto the pavement and not linger in the road.

Any other divergences in guide dog training when the USA and Britain are compared are of a relatively minor nature. The left turn is differently executed, but this is of little consequence as the end result is the same, with the British doing their right about threequarter turn, whilst the Americans face across the dog to the left before moving in that direction. Regarding equipment, the two harnesses are dissimilar. British and American schools are all financed by voluntary support. Government subsidies are few, except perhaps by way of waived dog taxes and concessionary fares on public transport. In Germany, Health Insurance agencies make provision for the acquisition of guide dogs.

World-wide, the aim of the guide dog movement is to provide blind individuals from all walks of life with a friendly and trusting animal which offers a measure of compensation for impaired standards of mobility, safety and independence. Wrapped up in the same canine bundle is happy and loyal companionship. Concerning the needs of the dog, there is now that indefinable but basic satisfaction derived by way of a rewarding working partnership with the human master, and being well looked after and cared for by that same person. Both in America and Britain, and many other countries, with regard to guide dog training and provision all of these factors are adequately met.